HISTORICAL ARCHAEOLOGY OF BAGAMOYO: EXCAVATIONS AT THE CARAVAN-SERAI

Felix Chami
Eliwasa Maro
Jane Kessy
Simon Odunga

Dar es Salaam University Press Ltd

Published in Tanzania by:
Dar es Salaam University Press Ltd.
P.O. Box 35182
Dar es Salam.

ISBN 9976 60 402 5

Copy-editing and book design: Bernhard J. Sanyagi

TABLE OF CONTENT

LIST OF FIGURES

PLATES

FOREWORD

The history of Bagamoyo begins with the period 1830 – 40. This was the result of the establishment of Zanzibar as the capital of the Oman Sultanate by Seyyid Said and the subsequent intensification of the slave and ivory trade. But this concept follows the foreign model that it was the Arab and Indian traders who supported and encouraged Sultan Seyyid to found Bagamoyo. However, it is important to underscore the point that trade and cultural interactions between the coast and the interior existed even before 1800 AD. Archaeologists interested in the rise of the Swahili culture and the ruined settlements of the East African Coast worked in the older sites such as Kaole, Kunduchi and Kilwa.

It was only in the year 2001 that some archaeological works were undertaken at caravan-serai in Bagamoyo historical area. The reasons for excavating at caravan-serai were to be able to provide knowledge about the functions and background of the site and to find out the existing oral tradition that the site had been used as a place to accumulate slaves from the interior before their last journey to the Zanzibar market is true.

The publication intends, therefore, to discuss the above and ultimately educate the public as to what might have been the functions and role of the caravan-serai in relation to trade caravans.

It is my hope that this publication will shed light on issues that have been taken for granted as facts. However, I wish to emphasize that this is only the beginning. I do hope that more excavation works will be undertaken in this area for further understanding and clarity on slavery in Tanzania in view of the rest of Africa.

In preparing this publication, both the director and department in general wish to acknowledge numerous colleagues particularly Prof. Felix Chami who was the leader of the excavation works and also supervised the writing of the manuscript. Ms Eliwasa Maro, Jane Kessy, Remigius Chami, Chediel Msuya, Simon Odunga and many whom I cannot mention by name. Particularly thanks go to the University of Dar-es-Salaam archaeology unit for agreeing to coordinate the works and the Swedish Government for sponsoring it. I am sure this publication will not only be a source of information on caravan-serai, but also an inspiration to the antiquities department staff, particularly those who participated.

Kamamba, D.M.K.
Director of Antiquity

_____

CHAPTER 1

INTRODUCTION

The excavations of the caravan-serai are the first known to be conducted in the historical town of Bagamoyo (Fig. 1 and 2). Archaeologists interested in the rise of the Swahili culture and the ruined monuments of the islands and the coast of East Africa laboured in the older sites such as Kaole and Kilwa. It was in the ruined settlements or in other non-monumental sites where the ancient history was thought to belong. Bagamoyo remained for them a historical town, flourishing in the 19th century with its rise and fall documented in the reports of explorers, missionaries and colonial archives. Recent interest in the conservation of the town, due to the role it played in the slave trade of the 19th century, has created a need to test the historical and oral records archaeologically.

Excavations at the Bagamoyo caravan-serai lasted twelve weeks, six in the year 2001 and the remaining six in 2002. This was a project directed by Prof. Chami with assistance from the members of the Antiquity Unit. The work was commissioned by the Antiquity Unit with financial support from the Embassy of Sweden.

First excavations, which took place between April and May 2001, examined the inside of the serai. The second season, August-September 2002, re-examined parts of the inside but with more emphasis on the area outside the walls of serai. The second season also coincided with the Bagamoyo World Heritage Conference with the aim of promoting the town to a World Heritage Site.

It should be noted at this juncture that the site of caravan-serai was considered important in the recent history of Bagamoyo as a place where slaves were accumulated after a difficult and exhausting journey from the deep interior of Africa. The last leg awaiting them was the voyage to Zanzibar where the international market was located. The role the town of Bagamoyo played in the 19th century in relation to the ivory and slave trade, the exploration of Africa and the spread of the coastal Swahili traditions to the heart of Africa will be discussed in the subsequent chapters. In recognition of such a role, the only place which would have assumed such importance, probably next to a palace and religious centre, would have been the caravansary or caravan-serai. In the history of the Middle East and Near East such places were used to lodge those involved in long- distance trade and the large compound within the centre would probably have provided space to accumulate bulk goods. The American Heritage Dictionary has defined caravan-serai as a large inn or hostelry. Understanding the history of a town's caravan-serai would therefore entail the understanding of the history of the town in terms of trade and hence its importance in relation to the larger regional and probably world economy.

One reason to excavate the Bagamoyo caravan-serai due to the lack of adequate written sources, was to provide knowledge about the function and background of the site in relation to the rest of the town. The monument, which was bought by the government from an individual for the purpose of conservation in 2001, thanks to the Swedish Embassy, needed to have its records put in order. Another reason was actually more academic: to find out if the oral tradition was right that the site had been used as a place to store slaves. As shown above, a caravan-serai would have acted as a hostel. The main story from oral traditions that the place had been used as a slave storage needed to be tested. Against that tradition is the argument by Areskough and Persson (1999: 93) that:

> The Caravan-Serai was built as an assembly point for arriving and departing caravans travelling to, and from, the interior of Tanzania. It also accommodated travellers engaged in the trade. It was here [that] the exchange of goods and enlistment for porters took place.

Indeed, in support of Areskough and Persson, a map of 1875 (Fig. 3), indicates that there was what is today identified as caravan-serai and another place near it, to the west, identified as the slave camp.

If, as had been thought, the place was used as a lodge for those involved in the caravans, then the archaeology of the place would find many more rooms than those seen standing today and the storey house in the middle would not have been there by the time of the caravans as the centre would have been a courtyard. The rooms would also have been better built and finished for the rich traders to stay there. The archaeology was also supposed to find more precious artifacts in the rooms and in the maiden. On the other hand, it was hypothesized that if the place had been used to accumulate slaves, then there would have been no need to overbuild the space inside the walls and hence not much structure would have been discovered by archaeological work apart from what is seen on the surface. Moreover, few artifacts would have been discovered in the excavations as slaves would have had no material belongings of their own. Probably what we would find are remains of pillars used to chain slaves and probably chains themselves as seen today in the slave market of Zanzibar.

This work, therefore, was aimed to put the Bagamoyo caravan-serai in a better historical context and illustrate its role and function using archaeological work. The work will first draw attention to the location of caravan-serai and Bagamoyo in general, then provide a short history of Bagamoyo, its relation to trade and exploration caravans and go on to describe the archaeological work done at the caravan-serai. A discussion and conclusion will follow.

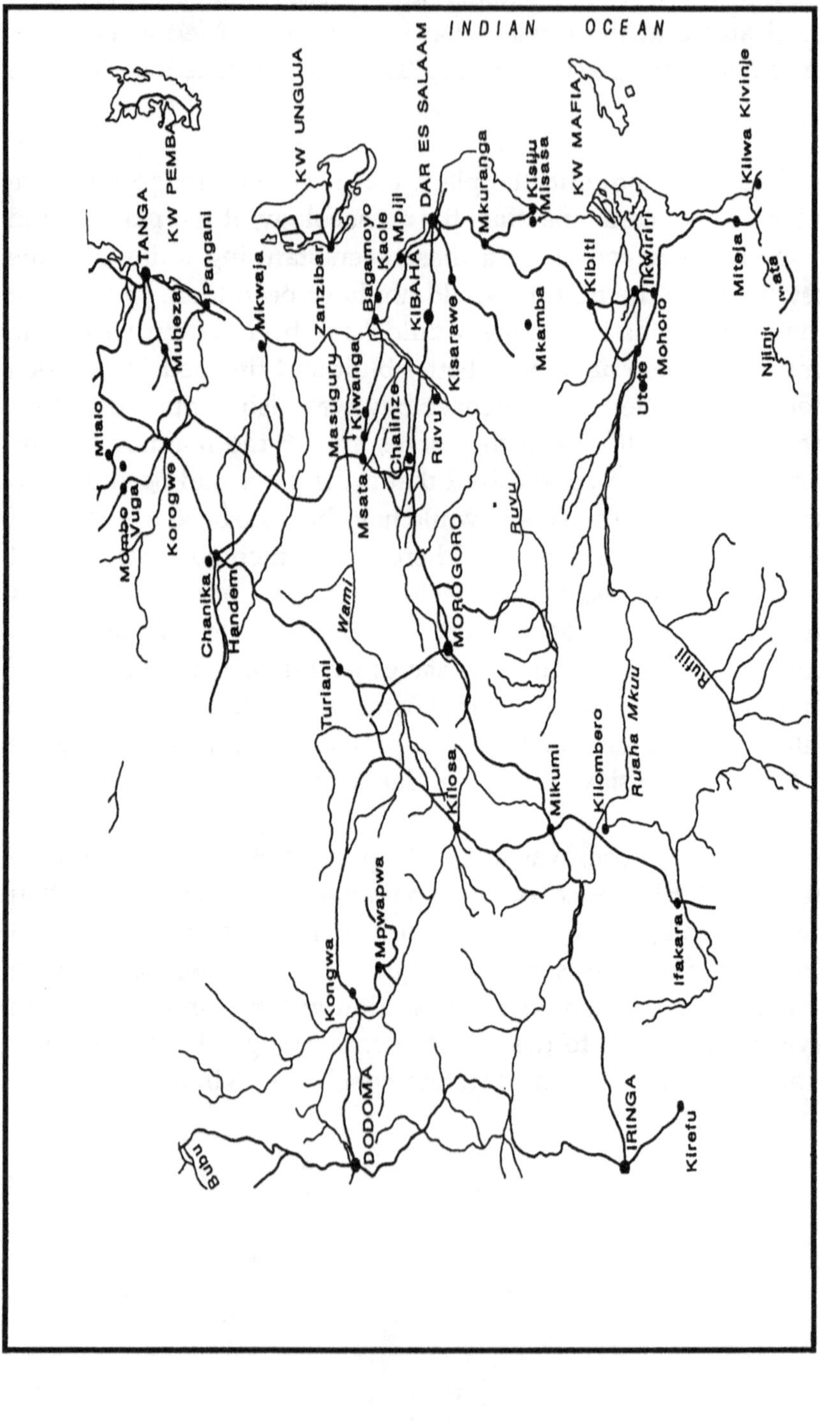

Fig. 1: *Tanzanian Central Coast and the Islands*

CHAPTER 2

LOCATION OF BAGAMOYO AND CARAVAN-SERAI

The geography of Bagamoyo has been described by Areskough and Persson (1999). The town is on latitude 6^0 5' and longitude 36^0 4'. It is about 70 km north of Dar-es-Salaam and about 40 km east of Zanzibar. The delta of the Ruvu River north and north-west and the wide river to the west makes the area of Bagamoyo appear as a peninsular (Fig. 1). Bagamoyo town is also located on an elevated marine terrace called Mtoni (Chittick 1962). This elevation is a product of tectonic forces which have warped the continental shelf between Zanzibar and mainland Tanzania (see Temple 1971). 4 km south of here, on the lower beach terrace, is found the older ruins of Kaole dating back to between the 12th and 18th century AD. It would seem that in recent times the coast around Bagamoyo has been affected by siltation some of which forms the sandy beaches of Bagamoyo town. This process is caused by the material brought by many small and large rivers empting into the ocean and winds reaching the central coast from the south-east dragging the sand further north along the beach (see Kwekason 2002).

The location of Bagamoyo town was probably determined mainly by its proximity to Zanzibar, which needed an entrëpot on the mainland. Among the competing localities for the entrëpot were Dar-es-Salaam/Kunduchi, Bagamoyo/Kaole and Saadani/ Pangani. It would seem that the Bagamoyo area was closer to Zanzibar and already had the traditional settlement of Kaole suggesting that there was a population concentration by the end of the 18th century (see Chami 2002a, b).

The climate of Bagamoyo is similar to that of the rest of the central coast including the islands. It is tropical, found within latitude 6°,5′ and longitude 39°, humid and hot. The annual average temperature is 26°C and the hottest period, December-March, is 32-35° C. The longer and heavy rainfall is between April and May and the shorter rains are between November and December falling between 508 and 1270 mm per year (see Morgan 1973; Chami 1994).

Caravan-serai during the 19th century and up to very recently, before the town was planned and expanded, was located outside the town centre, on the south-western part, about 400 meters from the Boma (Fig. 2). It was located in a farm probably belonging to Maghram, as Brown (1970: 76) reports that:

> Immediately after his arrival in the late 1850's, he began planting coconut trees, subsequently sold the fruit and invested in trading expeditions to the Ukami area.... By 1885, he had accumulated numerous slaves and extensive land holdings (his largest being the caravan stop Shamba Gonera).

Brown suggests that the farm would have been a few miles due west of Bagamoyo, suggesting that the present caravan-serai is not part of that farm as it was located about a hundred meters away from the town wall.

Today it is located along the new road going to the new market and bus stand as one comes from Dar-es-Salaam. For detailed location of caravan-serai in relation to other historic monuments see Areskough and Persson (1999).

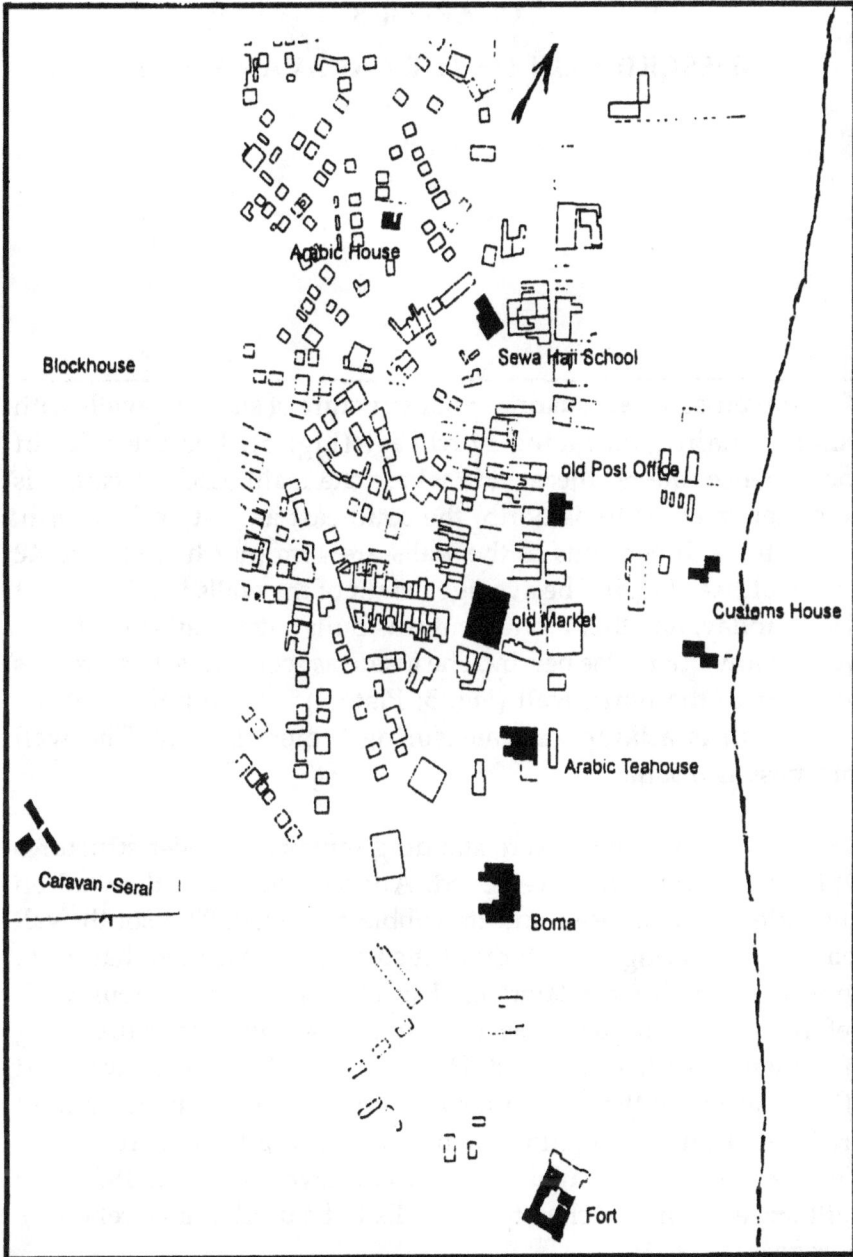

Fig. 2: *The historical town of Bagamoyo showing the caravan-serai on the southwest. Observe the fort to the south and customs house near the shoreline (After Areskough & Persson 1999)*

CHAPTER 3

DESCRIPTION OF THE CARAVAN-SERAI

Caravan-serai is a quadrangular structure of standing walls with the main gate facing northeast (Fig. 5). For the sake of convenience, the northeast side where the main gate is located is hereafter referred to as north, the southeast as east and so forth. The outside dimensions of the walls are 40m (north wall) and 42 (east wall)(see Fig.5). The average height of the walls is 2.86m. As it is seen today, no other monument was built outside attached to the walls or anywhere else nearby. The inside as seen today, has 8 rooms attached to the north wall (Fig. 5; Plate 1). At the middle of the north wall is a large gate measuring 3 meters wide. The wall thickness is 0.55m.

On the west side there were standing remains of toilet structures which have today been removed. A large portion of the wall on this side had collapsed and its rubble removed. The south wall remained standing. The study of it suggested that there had been windows which were later filled in to create a continuous wall. Before the excavations it was not easy to determine when the filling of the windows had occurred. However, the study of the wall and other features on that side of the monument showed the remains of brick, wall and foundations which, according to oral traditions, were said to have been built by a recent developer in the1950s. He built large rooms attached to the walls to be used as a warehouse/storage.

The east wall was more broken, but, unlike the west wall, having more parts standing. Most of its rubble had fallen inside and attached to the middle part is the later brick structure. In this wall the window spaces which, unlike those of the south wall, are less filled in. The window spaces clearly suggests that there had been rooms, similar to those on the north wall, attached to the east wall. A more focused study of the south wall also suggested that there had been a gate, later filled in, as wide as that of the north wall. As will be shown later, it had to await archaeological work to determine when the making and filling of the gate occurred.

At the centre of the courtyard stands the most impressive building in the area hereafter identified as the storey house (Plate 1a & b; Fig. 5). Its dimensions are 8.24m long and 12.94m wide. It is also built using coral rubble and lime, the upstairs having its floor supported by timber. The ground floor has 5 rooms and a narrow corridor. The upstairs has 3 rooms with a long balcony. It was not easy to determine the age of the house before excavations. At the time of the study the house was in a state of deterioration, the floor of the upstairs rooms had fallen down and the staircase was also in a state of collapse. In general, before renovations, the whole monument was a ruin.

The real surprising thing about the history of Bagamoyo is that few, if any at all, remember how the caravan-serai looked before 1950. One old man could only remember that at one time there had been many rooms in caravan-serai and another person remembers a developer who built the place using bricks. The only story shared by virtually everyone is that the place had housed slaves and that the road to Dar-es-Salaam passed near the southeast wall. This dearth of information about this monumental building of Bagamoyo would suggest that most knowledgeable people moved out to settle in other more prosperous towns such as Dar-es-Salaam and those remaining are newcomers. Alternatively, those remaining could also have been of a lower class not allowed at that time to access the monumental buildings. Another factor leading to the dearth of information could be the short-lived history of Bagamoyo which precluded proper writing of the town's history.

CHAPTER 4

A HISTORY OF BAGAMOYO

The ruins of Kaole are the oldest remains of a civilization on the central Tanzanian coast whose buildings were built using coral and lime now identify as of Swahili culture (Chami 1998; 2002a, b). Kaole dates between the 12/13th and the 18th century AD although the upper terrace near the ruins has remains showing occupation dating back to the 7th century AD. Prominent at the site today are many tombs, some still having pillars and bowl impressions of Chinese porcelain/celadon. Also found at the site are two mosques and two houses. One of the houses was discovered recently by this author (see Chami 2002b). Outside the Kaole conservation area is also the village of Kaole. The village has a port, not the same one as used by the pre-17th century Kaole community, and graves, some dating back to the 19th century AD.

On the other hand, the history of Bagamoyo begins from the mid-19th century when the town became the main gateway to the interior. However, the earliest available record of occupation is that of the late 18th century AD. According to Brown (1970: 71):

> The first major event in Bagamoyo's history dates back to the arrival of the Muslim Shomvi diwans. The earliest evidence of their presence is found in the town's cemeteries. Among more than forty tombs at Makaburini Mwana Makuka the only two legible dates are read as: A.H. 1208 (=A.D. 1793/94) and A.H. 1228 (=A.D. 1813). Surface finds of Chinese Ming dynasty blue and white pottery belong to this period.

The Shomvi Swahili clan is claimed to have founded towns between the Dar-es-Salaam area and Bagamoyo. The exact date of the Shomvi arrival on the central coast of Tanzania is not known.

Chittick (1970: 66), who does not declare the source of his information, claims that the Shomvi people were descendants of the Hatimi clan "who trace their ancestry back to a family from Barawa that settled at Kaole early in the seventeenth century." If that is the case, then the clan did not found Kaole because the site has archaeological records going back to the 12th century AD (see Chittick 1970; Chami 2002b). If one were to believe in Chittick's claim, the only cultural material remains that could be attributed to this group at Kaole could be the graves and the mosque on the eastern side of the site dating after AD 1600 to about 1750. However, there is no inscription, either in the ruins or in the modern village of Kaole, commemorating the settlement or the death of such people to enable historians to suggest that Kaole was the secondary dispersal point after the alleged Barawa nucleus area.

On the other hand, the earliest record of the Shomvi clan elsewhere is that found in Kunduchi, about 20 km north of Dar-es-Salaam, dating back to the early 18th century and probably slightly earlier (Sassoon 1966). The tombs commemorate the burial of the members of the ruling family, Sultan, of a Shomvi clan, claiming origin in Barawa (al Hatimi al Barawa). Chittick (1970: 68) has dated the mosque at Kunduchi back to the 15th century. If again this is correct, it would also imply, as in the case of Kaole, that the Shomvi clan did not found Kunduchi as claimed by oral traditions. If so then it would mean that the clan was on the central coast before the alleged 17th century AD suggesting that the Shomvi were just another Swahili clan of the central coast of Tanzania and their claim of origin in the north was meant to elevate their status given the racial divisions of the 17th-19th century. Since there is no evidence yet collected to corroborate Chittick's early date of the mosque, one can also assume that the mosque, like that of Kaole, was part of an earlier tradition, and if the Shomvis were immigrants they arrived on the central coast in the late 17th century for this is the time their dead started to be commemorated. Prof. Chami's attempts to interview some Shomvi families at Mpiji and Changwehela suggests that they are both Swahili and Zaramo for they speak both languages (Chami 1990). Indeed the survey of the population on the central coast by Speke (1863: 17) in the middle of the 19th century suggested that all settlements on the area between Dar-es-Salaam and Bagamoyo were occupied by Zaramo people whose leaders called Pazi were also Diwans.

Apart from the Mwanamakuka tomb inscriptions (see Plate 9a), no other written record about Bagamoyo is known about the early days of its development up to the middle part of the 19th century when travellers and missionaries reported about it. It is known that in those early days the Diwanates and Jumbeates of the Shomvi/Zaramo clans ruled Bagamoyo. However, their rule was guaranteed by paying tribute to the traditional Zaramo leader or Pazi who owned the land. It is not clear where the residence of Pazi was, but it could be hypothesized to have originally been at Kaole. In the middle of the 19th century Speke (1863) reports that the residence of the Zaramo Pazi was hidden in thick forest for strategic purposes. This hunch suggests that the Shomvi clan was just a new Swahili group who had been given land in Bagamoyo on which to settle by a traditional group probably based at Kaole then. According to Brown (1970: 72):

> The Wazaramo Pazi (the clan leaders) extracted tribute called kanda la pazi from the Shomvi diwans for the use of their land. This payment amounted to one third of the diwans' income from the sale of ivory, slaves, etc.

The fact that both Richard Burton (1872) and Speke (1863) do not mention Bagamoyo in their 1850s exploration reports would suggest that Bagamoyo was a small village and hence a suburb of Kaole. The later is reported by Burton as the gateway they used to the deep interior. If Bagamoyo had another name then the only possibility would be what is reported by Speke as Dege la Mhulo, a village near the delta of Ruvu River to be further discussed in chapter 6. In the story about the life of Tippu Tip, however, it is reported that Bagamoyo as a name and town did exist in the early 1850s as it was at Bagamoyo and Kilwa where the young Tippu Tip was allowed to visit "the customs' house, the slave dhows and barracoons where slaves were 'stored' waiting to be loaded on dhows" (Farrant 1975: 12). In the early 1850s, two renowned explorers, Abel and Nassoro (see Chapter 6), are reported to have passed through Bagamoyo (Gray 1957). It is also reported that in his accompanied trip to Tabora to visit his father before beginning his trading career in the mid-1850s, Tippu Tip passed through Bagamoyo (Farrant 1975: 17). We also saw in Chapter 2 that one, Maghram, arrived in Bagamoyo in the late 1850s.

Another side of the history of Bagamoyo pertains to the rise of the Pazi rulers of the Bagamoyo and Dar-es-Salaam region. It is the oral tradition which says that the Zaramo, the traditional ethnic group in this region, originated from the Kutu people of the Ruvu valley after their original leader, Pazi Kilama or Kilamia, assisted the communities of the coastal littoral fight off the Kamba invasion (Alpers 1969:49-50). It is the subsequent settlement of the Kutu warriors on the littoral which led to the modern Zaramo people. It is not known when this happened but Alpers (1969) puts it in the 18th century. The problem with this oral tradition is that it does not say who were the people who had settled on the littoral areas before them but only suggests that the Pazi conquest led the coastal towns into paying taxes to him for his protection. The word "Kilama" or "Kilamia" in some original Bantu language would mean to conquer and hence the story revolves around the hero: Pazi the conqueror. It is not clear if this occurred when Bagamoyo had been founded.

The history of Bagamoyo becomes clearer after the late 1860s when the missionaries had settled in the town and more so after 1870 when Sultan Majid, who had conceived Dar-es-Salaam as his new capital, died and the new ruler, Baragash, directed more attention to Bagamoyo. Whereas, as it will be shown later, most of pre-1970 caravan expeditions passed though Kaole, Kunduchi or Dar-es-salaam/Bommaji, Bagamoyo catered for most of the trade and exploratory caravans of post-1870. Within ten years the town had grown dramatically and, as will be shown, that is when the caravan-serai, the fort and customs houses were built (Brown 1970). Bagamoyo town was established as the indisputable entrepot of the mainland by the Zanzibar regime. According to Brown (1970) this is the time that many people of different Asiatic groups came to settle and build houses in Bagamoyo. The Christian missionaries had also acquired land and were settled there.

The power of the traditional Zaramo community in the area of Bagamoyo must have been enormous before this development because even at this period of Oman colonialism and Bagamoyo cosmopolitanism the traditional leadership continued claiming the ownership of the land of Bagamoyo. In 1868 they challenged the Sultanate's offer to give land to the Holy Ghost Fathers and in 1875 they organized an attack on Bagamoyo town (Brown 1970: 72-73).

Grievances of the traditional Zaramo people in Bagamoyo continued up to the time of the German East Africa Company between 1884/5 to 1889. "In April 1888 the Deutsch Oest-Africa Gesellschaft (DOAD) and Sayyid Khalifa, the recently enthroned Sultan of Zanzibar, signed a treaty granting the former the right to collect customs duties along the coastal stretch that included Bagamoyo"(Brown 1970:80). The Germans did not entertain negotiations with the Pazi as the Shomvi diwans and the Sultan representatives (liwali) had done before. They introduced new regulations which did not respect the ownership of the land by local people and German trade agents went into the interior to collect trade commodities without paying tribute to the Diwans or Pazi (see Henshel 2000:26-27; Versteijnen 1975: 24-25; Brown 1970: 80).

The Wazaramo people led by Bushiri, now with the support of the Shomvi and other nearby ethnic groups, launched a war against the Germans. "This armed resistance of 1888-9, misnamed the 'Arab Revolt,' involved the whole of the coastal region that the Germans were trying to bring under control" (Sutton 1970: 6). The Arab traders apparently supported the revolt against the Germans. However, the organization and the spirit behind the revolt belonged to the local people of Bagamoyo area and not to Arabs who did not belong to the region. It was the Shomvi Swahili clan, who had paid tribute to the Zaramo leader for staying and trading in Bagamoyo who supported their African colleagues against the Germans. The main evidence that the Shomvi were coastal Africans, and not Arabs, is that the names of their diwans, who fought alongside Bushiri and were hanged together, are of Bantu/Swahili language. The diwanis' names included Mbomboma, Marera, Makanda, Pori,

Marara, Simbambili, and Jehasi (Brown 1970:81; Henshel 2000: 26-27). Richard Burton (1872: 424-425) observed that, while the Swahili people adopted Muslim names for religious purposes, in their African scenes they were identified with their traditional names.

The Germans won the war, but were affected psychologically in their plan to rule the territory from Bagamoyo. Only two years after the Bushiri war, the Germans decided to move their capital 70 km south of Bagamoyo to Dar-es-Salaam. One major reason noted by historians for the capital's movement is that Mzizima was a protected bay with deep water. However, that harbour place, first conceived by Sultan Majid in 1862 as a "house of peace"- hence Dar-es-Salaam (Sutton 1970) as it is known today- cost the Germans large sums of money to deepen the channel to the bay. Reports of 1866-1888 suggest that the channel was dangerous, the land was unhealthy and no labourers or slaves could be kept in the area (See *Tanganyika Notes and Records* 1970: 201-203).

It may be deemed controversial if one were to argue that the main reason for the capital's movement was the effect of the Bushiri war. The war had destroyed most of the town and created unprecedented enmity between the local people and the new rulers. The hanging of their beloved leaders enflamed their hearts and was a major psychological deterrent for the new colonizers to engage amicably with the locals. It was similar local resistance to foreign rule from Bagamoyo/Kaole that had caused Sultan Majid to develop Dar-es-Salaam rather than Bagamoyo and not due to a good harbour:

> There were other reasons why Majid should have preferred to found a new city at Dar-es-Salaam rather than take over Bagamoyo, closer to Zanzibar and already the most prosperous town of the Mrima. While it enjoyed the commercial connection with Zanzibar (and was in a way parasitic upon this), there were well established local interests at Bagamoyo represented by the Shomvi diwan, as well as the surrounding Zaramo and their pazi (leaders), who would resist direct control by the Sultan (Sutton 1970:4).

When the German East Africa Company was replaced by the German government administration after the 1888/9 war, the decision to move the capital to Dar-es-Salaam was effected in 1891. Bagamoyo was now to be second to Dar-es-Salaam, and a few years later to fall into ruin only to be rescued in the 1980s when it was made a seat for district administration and more recently in an effort to declare it a World Heritage site.

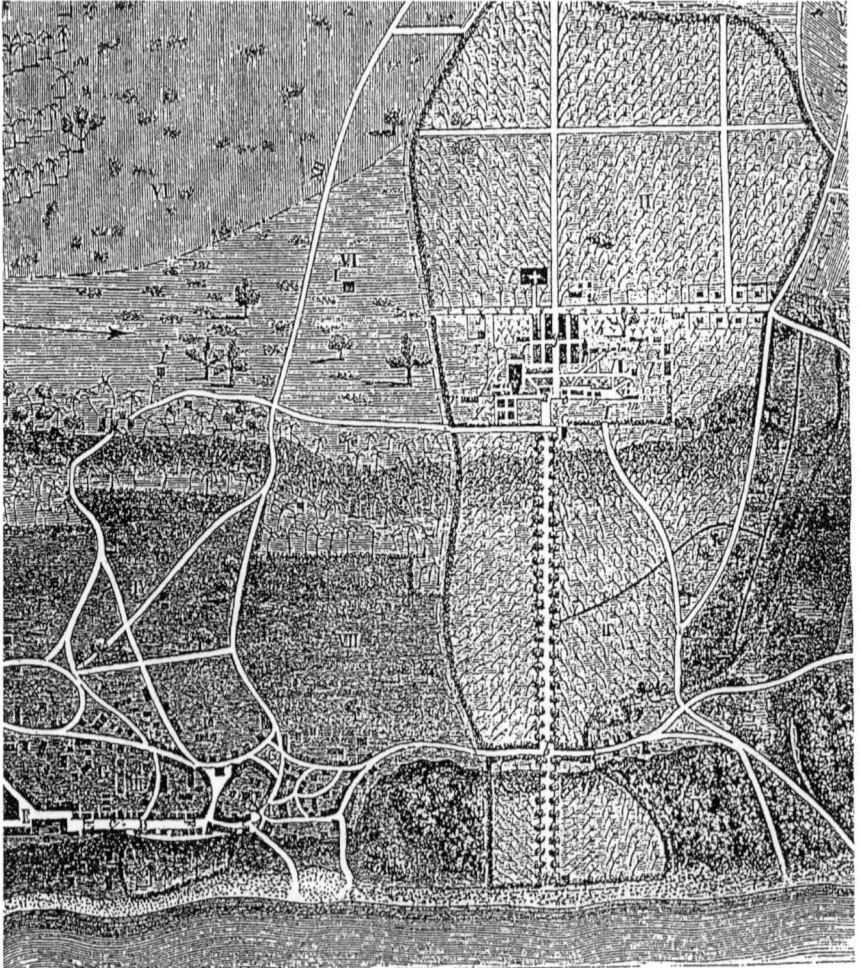

Fig. 3: A Bagamoyo map of 1873. **H** stands for caravan-serai and **i** for slave camp
(*Source*: Roman Catholic Museum files)

CHAPTER 5

THE FALL OF KAOLE AND THE RISE OF BAGAMOYO

The fall of Kaole, as evidenced by the ruins, and the rise of both the modern Kaole village and the town of Bagamoyo, has been explained mainly by using environmental factors. Brown (1970:70) has argued that the growth of the mangrove forest or siltation of the old harbour, the fall in the water table and siltation of the wells are among the factors that led to the decline of Kaole. Another factor discussed is an economic one: which, according to Brown (1970: 70), includes:

> A combination of natural disasters and economic change probably encouraged a shift of population to Bagamoyo. What made the latter site attractive was the fertility of its immediate hinterland and its proximity to the rice-producing Kingani (Ruvu) River region. Since Bagamoyo had the potential to feed an expanding population and to be utilized as a base for supplying caravans to the interior, the town soon eclipsed its declining neighbour.

It has indeed been shown that between AD 1500 and 1800 there could have been a drop in the sea level which caused the protected harbour of Kaole on the southern side of the site to become inaccessible (Chami 1994, 2002b). In the meantime, siltation of the area around the Kaole Peninsular occurred due to processes explained elsewhere (Kwekason 2002). These may have led to the growth of the mangroves, which now lay siege to the peninsular. Also the process which involved the lifting and warping of the ocean could also have affected the water table of the place as indeed observed by the empty wells once used to cater for the ruined town of Kaole. The question, however, is whether the move of the harbour to the present village would not have been a more satisfactory measure rather than the move 5km to the north. It will be shown that the port of Kaole was still in use competing with Bagamoyo in the 1850s. It is also likely that because Kaole and Bagamoyo were both within walking distance of the Kingani valley, the agricultural advance claimed above for the latter may not be a serious factor that would cause a traditional town to collapse.

Re-examination of the history of Bagamoyo would suggest that socio-political factors may have played a major role in determining its rise. It was the arrival of the Omanis with their base in Zanzibar and the arrival of the new Swahili Shomvi clan in the Bagamoyo area, both occurring in the late 17th and early 18th century, that catalysed the rise of Bagamoyo at the expense of Kaole. The Omanis had been invited by some Swahili people to come and help expel the Portuguese from East Africa at the end of the 17th century (Vernet 2002). Having accomplished that they stayed and used force to rule the Swahili coast. During the 1830s Zanzibar became the Omani capital stimulating trade and production along the central coast of East Africa. The discussion on the arrival of the Shomvi has been conducted above.

Historical experience shows that when a new people or power arrives in an area with a traditional flourishing centre several trends occur. First, if the local population and the newcomers prefer not to mix, the newcomers may be allocated their own land slightly away from the traditional cultural centre. If the newcomers are more enterprising or more powerful economically their new settlement will become more eminent, leading to the decay of the old traditional centre. A good example of this is the report in the Kilwa Chronicle. The new Shirazi clan was given the island of Kilwa by the traditional leader for their settlement. Since the Shirazi leader did not like to mix with the traditional leader, the latter and his people moved out of the island to a traditional royal seat on the mainland side. Since the Shirazi leader married the daughter of the local leader, the local leader passed his royal powers to his grandson who was the product of that mixed marriage. Since this grandson continued to reside on the island of Kilwa, becoming the King of both the Shirazi immigrants and of the rest of the people of Kilwa, the island flourished as the new centre (see Nurse and Spear 1985: 70-72).

There are other examples of recent colonial history, which are yet to be published. One that springs to mind is the coming of Lutheran Missionaries to the Machame area in Kilimanjaro. The tradition holds that the King of Machame, afraid to refuse the missionaries a place to settle due to the Germans' power in the region, offered the missionaries a place near a traditional burial area, expecting the spirits to deal with them squarely. The missionaries built a Christian centre in the area including a church, hospital and school facilities. This became the new centre as opposed to the King's palace. Another example of a similar kind is that of Roman military centres in many parts of ancient Europe which were first established away from the traditional towns because of their initial military function. These soon developed other features of centrality (Renfrew 1975:32).

One probable scenario relates to possible future alternatives explanation for what happened in the Kaole-Bagamoyo area. The coming of the Shomvi people, although being invited, were allocated land 5km north of the traditional settlement of Kaole on condition that they would pay taxes for the use of the land and for trading. Since, as was shown earlier, the Zanzibar sultanate was uneasy with the power of the traditional rulers in Kaole, it is likely that they favoured the new settlement which in effect overthrew the traditional one.

Second, and a corollary to the first, is when there is local resistance to a powerful coloniser. Colonisers control the centre of a traditional settlement by usurping all political powers of the traditional rulers and by controlling the economy. Resistance by the local population leads to antagonism and hence regular conflicts. Consequently, one of two things may happen. First, the local elite may decide to found a new location from which to run their operations because of the control of their centre by colonisers. This new location may develop to rival or succeed the old one. Second, if the antagonism is too obstructive for the colonizers to operate in the traditional centre, they may decide themselves to develop a new centre or support the foundation of one near the traditional centre in order to be able to secure themselves and monitor the affairs of the traditional centre.

Several examples exist for the two sub-models. When the Portuguese entered the waters of eastern Africa they found a brisk trade going on between the Swahili towns. Gold was among the trade items most wanted by the Portuguese in that trade network. They proceeded to attack the Swahili towns, particularly Sofala, Kilwa and Mombasa, and controlled them. It was during this period that the Swahili traders developed new trading centres away from the traditional ones to avoid the power of the new rulers. Angoche and Kilwa Kivinje were developed for Sofala and Kilwa respectively (Datoo 1975; Pikirayi 2003). Because of the failure of the newcomers to deal with antagonism at the old centres we have the Germans in Tanganyika locating some of their centres away from the traditional ones which had revolted against their rule. Moshi of Kilimanjaro was built a few kilometers south-west of Old Moshi by the British after Meli, whose father had given the Germans a base in his capital, resisted German rule (Gwasa 1969). The move of the German capital from Bagamoyo to Dar-es-Salaam is likely to be another example of failure by the Germans to cope with local resistance especially after hanging Bushiri and his collaborators for resisting their rule.

An indication suggesting this explanation, especially part two of it, the Kaole-Bagamoyo area is the placement by the sultan of Zanzibar of a Baluchi barracks/garrison at Kaole from time immemorial suggesting that the traditional town was put under the control of the Zanzibar sultanate while encouraging the growth of Bagamoyo or even Dar-es-Salaam at the time of Majid.

> ...Kaole was later selected as a military and administrative centre by the sultan of Zanzibar. A resettlement of the site by the Sultan's Baluchi troops resulted in a gradual population increase throughout the eighteenth century (Brown 1970: 70).

The garrison functioned up to about 1870 when Bagamoyo emerged as an indubitable entrepot for the coast of East Africa. Burton (1872) reported of a garrison from where five Baluchis were recruited in the mid -1850s. Actually the garrison could have provided "about a hundred additional Baluchis to escort" the caravan for the first few miles (Simpson 1975: 14).

This historical fact suggests that the Omanis had been resisted by the traditional centre of Kaole. Whereas Kaole was clamped down by the use of military force, Bagamoyo was encouraged to grow as a new centre leading to the development of its port and opening up of its caravan route. It has been shown that, despite this clamping down of the traditional centre, Kaole, continued resisting. It was this reality which made Majid choose Dar-es-Salaam rather than Bagamoyo as his new capital in the 1860s.

> There were other reasons why Majid should have preferred to found a new city at Dar-es-Salaam rather than take over Bagamoyo...While it enjoyed the commercial connection with Zanzibar (and was in a way parasitic upon this), there were well established local interests at Bagamoyo represented by the Shomvi diwan, as well as the surrounding Zaramo and their pazi (leaders), who would resist direct control by the Sultan (Sutton 1970).

If the building of Dar-es-Salaam as a new capital had been successful it would have led to the abandonment of the Bagamoyo project. It was the succeeding Sultan Baragash after 1870, who continued with the Bagamoyo project, abandoning Dar-es-Salaam.

Scholars have also recognised trade realignment as another important factor which contributed to the shift in settlements. If a port of trade (see Hodges 1988: 52-55) or a gateway community (Hirth 1978: 37-38) loses its dendritic network due to war, exhaustion of resources or change in trade route then decline ensues. (Datoo 1975: 86-97) has attributed the demise of earlier East African coastal ports to this factor. One best example offered is that of disturbances in the Zimbabwe plateau which led to the rise of Monomutapa centre away from Great Zimbabwe. Ports of trade on the Mozambican coast had to realign to this change (also see Pikirayi 2003). This factor, however, does not hold much water in explaining why Kaole centre moved to Bagamoyo. The two centres are only 5km apart and they share the same hinterland and trade route to the interior.

In conclusion, it was the ingenuity of the Shomvi people, coupled with the resistance to Omani colonization, that led to the rise of Bagamoyo as a town. Consequently Kaole declined. Bagamoyo became an alternative port for traders who did not want to struggle with Pazi for permission to trade and settle in Kaole. The rise of Zanzibar as the capital of Omani brought further deterioration to Kaole. The sultanate would favour the neutral affairs of the new Bagamoyo town rather than operating within a traditional and conservative Kaole. The paying of much more attention to Bagamoyo by the Zanzibar sultanate, more so from 1970s, made it the unchallenged entrepot. The arrival of Arabs, Asiatic people and Europeans in Bagamoyo caused the town to become cosmopolitan (Brown 1970: 76). The fort and the caravan-serai were built.

CHAPTER 6

BAGAMOYO AND THE DEEP INTERIOR OF AFRICA: TRADE AND EXPLORATION

The growth of Bagamoyo in the 19th century coincided with the flowering of trade in the Indian Ocean after the collapse of a similar occurrence at the end of the 15th century AD (Kusimba 1999; Sinclair and Hakansson 2000). European expansion over all waters of the world from the 16th century led to a demand for mapping parts of the continents for the purpose of economic and political hegemony of the western powers. At the same time the growth of the Oman power in the Indian Ocean, which occurred after driving out the Portuguese force from East Africa after AD1698, created an economic opportunity for the Arabs and Indians to attend to the trade demands of East Africa, probably more so after Seyyid Said visited Zanzibar in 1828 and after 1840 when he had established Zanzibar as his capital (Alpers 1969). These developments stimulated the growth of trading ports on the mainland between Tanga and Kilwa. The ports acted as a gateway to the deep interior of Africa (Alpers 1969; Simpson 1975)

It should be noted here that European individuals sponsored by different companies and governments had been travelling through Africa since AD 1500. They had been establishing colonies like that of the Cape founded by the Dutch, and Mozambique and Angola formed by the Portuguese. Despite these colonies, reconnaissance of the deep of Africa had to await the second part of the 19th century. Simpson (1975) has shown that this task had to be accomplished by people from different backgrounds, including "explorers and scientists, missionaries and philanthropologists, traders and settlers and eventually, as European rule was established in Africa, administrators and soldiers" (Simpson1975:1).

Due to different problems, including lack of navigable rivers and failure of draught animals to survive disease, sub-equatorial Africa became difficult to explore. The 19th century saw an improvement in the technical and scientific means to explore after the industrial revolution occurred in Europe. Regular sailings, due to the appearance of steamships, facilitated regular supplies to the interior expeditions, including guns and medicines.

Despite the late European exploration of the deep interior of Africa, the Nyamwezi and other people of the interior had been in contact with the coastal people of East Africa from time immemorial. Knowledge existed on the coast of the deep interior of Africa, of its great lakes and rivers (see Gray 1957; Wheatley 1975). After the establishment of the Arab/Oman rule on the coast of East Africa from the 18th century, both Arabs and Swahili travellers and traders explored the interior more regularly. This was also augmented by regularly organised caravans by the people of the interior to the coast, i.e. the Nyamwezi. The proximity of Bagamoyo/Kaole to Zanzibar may have led to the concentration of traders in the area and hence the growth of large settlements.

PRE-EUROPEAN EXPLORATION VIA BAGAMOYO/KAOLE

The area of Kaole-Bagamoyo must have played a significant role in providing a link between the rest of the coast of East Africa and its deep interior, probably to the Great Lakes Region, before the advent of the European exploration in the 1850's. Simpson (1975) has mentioned some archaeological indications suggesting such a link with the Nyamwezi people although not through the Bagamoyo/ Kaole area. The archaeology of Kaole itself would suggest some contact with the northern highlands of Tanzania in the evidence of a volcanic stone from a context dating back to the 15th century AD (Chami 2002).

There is also some historical evidence suggesting knowledge of the interior and the Great Lakes Region by the coastal people from about the 14th century. Wheatley (1975) has a Chinese map of that period showing the lakes of East Africa and the Nile. The map was made when the Swahili trade was at its peak in the 13th –15th century before the invasion of Portuguese and other European powers. Old research in the Great Lakes Region has found beads of Indian origin in archaeological contexts dating back to the 14th century (Connah 1996). Recent works are also finding coastal materials like shells and glass beads of the same time period as far as Kilimanjaro/Tanga border (Waltz-*pers.comm*) and Iringa (Msemwa-pers. Com.). This would suggest that large settlements such as Kaole had been linked to the heart of Africa before the 16th century.

Gray (1957) has shown that from about 1800 the Oman Sultanate, then having a governor in Zanzibar, had encouraged and sponsored exploratory expeditions into the heart of Africa. The purpose was to know the source of ivory brought to the coast by the Nyamwezi traders who are alleged to have reached the coast in about 1800 (Alpers 1969). However, in Buganda, the Swahili trade goods are reported there from 1763 during the reign of Kabaka Suna-1 (Gray 1957) and the archaeological record points to the 17th century as the earliest Swahili contact (Posnansky 1975) suggesting that the Nyamwezi traders or others had contacted the coast earlier than 1800. The material items probably originating from the Swahili coast include beads, cowries, ceramics, cloths and copper objects (Posnansky 1975: 218). The Zanzibar Sultanate or other coastal authorities had probably been indirectly sending presents to African rulers in the deep interior as early as the mid-18th century. Such presents were used as a sign of friendship encouraging explorations to reach deep into Africa as far as Buganda and Angola on the Atlantic coast.

The earliest recorded traders and explorers include two Khoja brothers who were known to have reached Lake Tanganyika in 1825. It is not reported if they took off from Bagamoyo/Kaole area. Another one is a Zanzibar-born Nyamwezi, called Leif bin Said, reported to have reached Lake Tanganyika in 1831. In 1841-42, Mohammed *bin* Salih and Suleiman *bin* Nassor are reported to have gone through Lake Tanganyika to the modern Zambia (Gray 1957).

In the 1830s, one Muhammed *bin* Juma, the renowned Tippu Tip's father, had also established residence in Kazé at Tabora in the Kingdom of Fundikira. From that base, where he was married to Fundikira's daughter, he had been trading all the way west to central Africa (Farrant 1975).

The most interesting explorer is Said *bin* Habib el-Afif who travelled in about 1844, probably passing through Bagamoyo area with the purpose of exploring the deep interior of Africa to Central Africa and beyond. His expedition, which lasted 16 years, pioneered a survey of those areas visited by Dr. David Livingstone in modern Zambia. He reached Luanda on the Atlantic coast three times, probably being the earliest known by name to have crossed Africa (Gray 1957). In his later years of travel, he met Dr. Livingstone at Linyati, on the Zambezi River. Dr. Livingstone described him as a slave trader.

Other traders/explorers who reached the Atlantic coast from the Bagamoyo coast in 1851 include Abdel and Nassoro. For the first time in the known history Bagamoyo is mentioned as a caravan terminal.

It has been noted before that Bagamoyo as a place first appears in the historical records in about 1850. It has been argued earlier that it was not a port of significance in the 1850s for there is only one reported expedition that passed through Bagamoyo: that of Abdel and Nassoro. Another expedition of the pre-European exploration period, led by Musa Mazrui in 1844, passed with a company of the first European to have aimed at crossing Africa from the Indian to the Atlantic Ocean, a Frenchman called Mizrain, at a place near the Ruvu Delta called "Dege la Mhulo" (Gray 1957: 234). This was a settlement north of Kaole. It is questionable whether this was the same settlement as Bagamoyo. In that expedition Mizrain was left behind in the same settlement and believed to have been murdered later.

In this pre-European exploration period, reliable descriptions of landscapes such as Ruwenzori and waters like Nyanza/Victoria and the Nile had been reported. Among the people known to have had this knowledge include Musa Mazrui, reporting from about 1842 and Ahmed bin Ibrahim, Kyera and Amulane in the 1850's (Gray 1957).

It should also be noted here that the pre-European explorers and traders had managed to introduce Islam to the interior of East Africa by at least 1800, partially from Bagamoyo. This was done by introducing trade posts such as Kazé in Tabora. It was at these posts that local communities were converted. One example is that of the King of Buganda, Kabaka Suna II, who was converted to Islam in the early 19th century (Gray 1957). When the first missionaries reached the interior kingdoms they found Swahili Muslims in the residences of the Kings of various kingdoms, including Kimweri of Usambara and those of Kilimanjaro from before 1844 (Gwasa 1969).

EUROPEAN EXPLORATION VIA BAGAMOYO

The wave of European exploration began from 1850's when missionaries and travellers aimed to establish knowledge of the interior of Africa (see Fig. 4). Whereas Bagamoyo played an invaluable role for the European expeditions beginning from Zanzibar, not all explorers took off from Bagamoyo for the interior. Only those expeditions taking off and ending at Bagamoyo are of our concern in this work.

The earliest recorded attempt by European explorers through Bagamoyo is that of Mizrain in 1844. This Frenchman had the intention of crossing Africa from the Indian Ocean. As noted earlier Mizrain did not go beyond Bagamoyo area where he was later murdered.

The next recorded expedition by Europeans through the modern Bagamoyo area is that of Richard Burton and John Speke in 1857-59. This expedition is reported to have passed through Kaole which as noted earlier is only 5km south of Bagamoyo. This expedition of

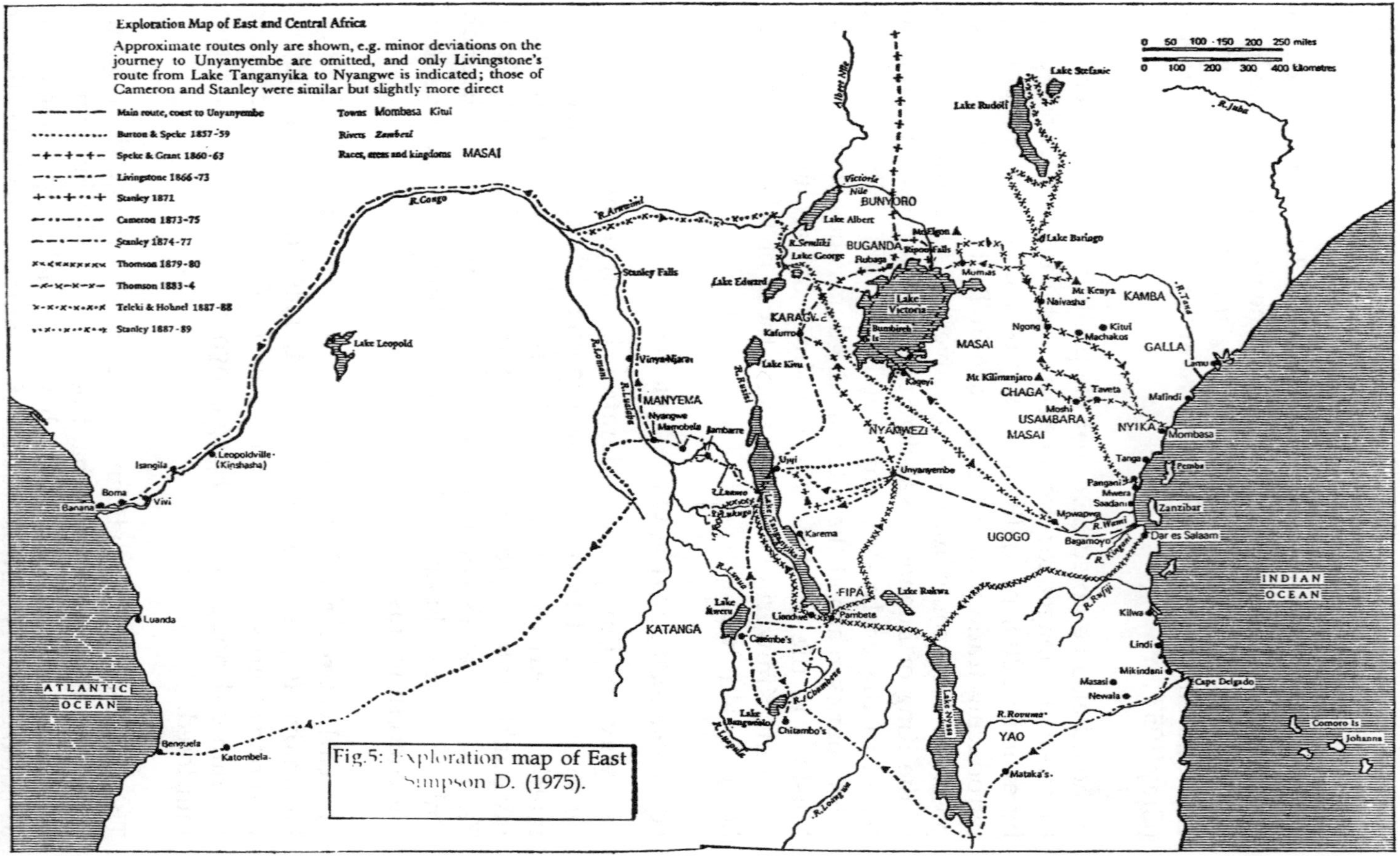

Exploration Map of East and Central Africa

Approximate routes only are shown, e.g. minor deviations on the journey to Unyanyembe are omitted, and only Livingstone's route from Lake Tanganyika to Nyangwe is indicated; those of Cameron and Stanley were similar but slightly more direct

——	Main route, coast to Unyanyembe	Towns	Mombasa Kisui
·········	Burton & Speke 1857-59	Rivers	Zambezi
-+-+-+-	Speke & Grant 1860-63	Races, areas and kingdoms	MASAI
++++++	Livingstone 1866-73		
+-+-+-+	Stanley 1871		
·-·-·-·	Cameron 1873-75		
-------	Stanley 1874-77		
x-x-x-x	Thomson 1879-80		
x-x-x-x	Thomson 1883-4		
x-x-x-x	Teleki & Hohnel 1887-88		
·-··-··-	Stanley 1887-89		

Fig. 5: Exploration map of East [...] Simpson D. (1975).

170 people had its caravan leaving Kaole with eight Baluchi escorting for the whole journey, but with about "one hundred additional Baluchis" (Simpson 1975:14). The purpose of Burton's expedition was to establish the source of the Nile.

After exploring Lake Tanganyika, Speke travelled to the Mwanza area where he saw Lake Nyanza, which he later coined Victoria, and speculated it to be the source of the Nile. His report was not accepted by Burton and hence sparked a controversy in Britain. This led to Speke's 1860 expedition.

James Grant accompanied Speke in the expedition of 1860. The success of this expedition also depended a lot on experienced Africans, both men and women, including Bombay, Mabruki, Frij, Uledi and Sikujua, Kahala, M'Essu and Faida respectively. From Bagamoyo, Speke's caravan passed through Tabora, Karagwe, Buganda, and Bunyoro reaching Cairo in April of 1864. It was from this expedition that modern Europeans first knew about the source of the Nile. This expedition also provided knowledge for the Europeans of the kingdoms about the Great Lakes Region.

It should be noted here that the failure by Speke's team to explore the point where the Nile enters and exits Lake Albert left a gap in the knowledge about the source of the Nile. Samuel Baker, who had been exploring the Nile from the north, met Speke at Gondokoro in southern Sudan, and continued south at that controversial point where the Nile exits Lake Albert. The expedition by David Livingstone, which did not pass through Bagamoyo, was partially meant to solve the Nile riddle as central African rivers, now known to be tributaries of the river Congo, were then speculated to continue north to fill the Nile.

Although Dr. Livingstone did not go through Bagamoyo, Henry Stanley's expedition to look for him passed Bagamoyo in 1871. Among legendary people recruited to assist Stanley were Bombay and Mabruki who accompanied Speke to Cairo. Dr. Livingstone was met at Ujiji.

Another important role played by Bagamoyo was that of being a passage for the body of Livingstone who died in Central Africa in May 1873. His loyal followers, Chuma and Susi, (and others) carried his body through central Tanzania to Bagamoyo, hence to Zanzibar and England. It should be noted here that the monuments in Bagamoyo commemorating that event have a colonial bias. It is time these were rephrased to read: "Here is where Chuma and Susi (and others) passed carrying the body of Dr. David Livingstone to Zanzibar and England." The passage episode took place in Bagamoyo in February 1874. However, Father Henschel of the Catholic church at Bagamoyo has stated that the commemoration now found at Bagamoyo refers to the door frame, now part of the house in Bagamoyo, through which Livingstone's body was passed at Ujiji.

Another important expedition passing through Bagamoyo is that of Verney Cameron of 1873-75 with the purpose of crossing Africa to the Atlantic Ocean. It has been noted that this kind of expedition by European explorers had already been accomplished by Swahili and Arab traders. Again the success of this mission depended very much on the experienced Africans led by Bombay. The expedition landed at Luanda in modern day Angola.

In 1874 Henry Stanley returned to Bagamoyo to launch an expedition aimed at establishing "detailed configuration of Lakes Tanganyika and Victoria, the outlet of Lake Tanganyika and the nature of the river system of the western portion of central Africa" (Simpson 1975:114). Once again, the success of this mission depended on experienced Africans including Mabruki and Mama Sera. This mission sailed around Lake Victoria, being the first recorded European sailor on the lake. Lake Edward was also viewed for the first time by Europeans. It was also confirmed that the central African rivers contributed to the Congo River. The expedition also resurveyed Lake Tanganyika and followed the Congo River to the Atlantic Ocean. The expedition ended in 1877.

The expeditions of Tippu Tip in central Africa, in most cases carried out *via* Bagamoyo, should also be mentioned here. These took place between the 1860s and 1880s. Tippu Tip conquered most kingdoms in central Africa and was the first person from the Swahili and European worlds to have had details of central Africa including the Congo basin. His experience assisted Livingstone, Cameroon and Stanley in their various efforts to map the deep regions of Africa. Indeed, Stanley organised a joint expedition with Tippu Tip in the late 1880s, during which time Tippu Tip was made both the ambassador or governor of the Congo region by the Zanzibar Sultanate and latter by the Belgians.

It should be noted here that the 1880's saw the European powers scrambling for Africa. Various expeditions by explorers, missionaries and traders had brought into being agreements both real and fake between European individuals, i.e. Carl Peters and African rulers (Gwasa 1969). Bagamoyo continued to play a key role as a terminal for the deep interior trade up to the early 1890's. In about 1886 Germany had claimed the East African territory later to be called Tanganyika, with boundaries outlined in various European treaties of that time (see Gwasa 1969: 11). The German's colonial interest in Tanganyika were represented by Deutsch Oest Africa, which was given the role of trading and exploiting various resources for Germany. All these initial colonial activities were run from Bagamoyo up to 1891 when the capital was moved to Dar-es-Salaam under the German Government rule.

Mention must also be made of the role of Bagamoyo in the spread of Christianity to the deep interior of Africa. Travellers/explorers such as Livingstone and Stanley had also taught Christianity to those who came close to them. For instance, Stanley made a great effort to see that the Buganda royalty, which was already Islamic by his time, was converted to Christianity. Darlington Scorpion Maftaa was given the role of teaching Christianity to Kabaka Mutesa. He translated the Bible into Kiswahili (Gray 1957). Kabaka Mutesa renounced Islam in favour of Christianity.

Probably another main role played by Bagamoyo is the spread of

Christianity to the whole of what became Tanganyika. The first Christian station in modern Tanzania and its interior, and indeed the first Catholic mission in mainland East Africa was that of Bagamoyo, founded in 1868 (for conspectus see Versteijnen 1968). By the 1880s other Christian groups, i.e. London Missionary Society, had reached Lake Tanganyika from Bagamoyo (see Farrant 1975).

CHAPTER 7

EXCAVATIONS OF THE CARAVAN-SERAI

PHASE ONE

a) Survey

The first task handled before excavation was to survey the town from the Bagamoyo College of Arts in the south to the Roman Catholic church in the north and from the shore to the road leading to Kiwangwa on the west. As was suggested before, the town of Bagamoyo was subjected to archaeological research for the first time and nothing was known about the real beginning of the settlement before mid-19th century when it is mentioned for the first time in the historical records.

The survey of the southern part, extending south-east and south from the caravan-serai to the higher elevated terrace at the edge of which are located the post office (and its tower), football ground and the newly planned upper-class quarters, were found cultural layers of an older settlement dating back to the 16th and 17th century, elsewhere known as Post Swahili (PS) tradition. The materials included pottery decorated on the neck using an instrument with four prongs dragged in a waving manner to create wave lines and also stamped to create a comb-stamped band. The core of this culture has been established in the south in the Rufiji region (see Chami 2001). This pottery has been found in the upper levels of the Kaole ruins associated with European beads, suggesting the date of post AD 1500. In the escarpment east of the football ground touching the road passing the Art College to Kaole, extending to the police station, was found a concentration of this pottery in association with abundant marine shells.

Examining the ditch then being dug to drain water from the market and bus stand, pottery of the same tradition was discovered in parts of the town via the front of caravan-serai and the post office. Four (4) potsherds of the earlier Triangular Incised Ware (TIW), a tradition dating back to between AD 600 and 900, were also collected. It should be noted that Kaole is the closest area known to have had the largest concentration of this cultural material, including many trade goods, suggesting that the Bagamoyo area could have been the periphery of this centre with only a few houses. The find of such a small number of TIW pottery could also be explained by movement of soil from a TIW site to the Bagamoyo area for the purpose of construction. Red/brown sandy soils, in which TIW sites are known to have been associated, sometimes mixed with hard materials such as pottery, coral stones and shells were used by later settlers to floor and plaster their houses and even gravel roads (see Chami 2002b). However, the TIW potsherds were not found in association with anything else that could be used to suggest their transportation to the find spot.

The other part of the town which seems to have been occupied before the 18th century is the area near the edge of the Mtone Terrace, before sloping down to the Beach Terrace where are located monuments such as the Mwanamakuka graves, the Fort and the Boma. On that cliff one can find PS pottery protruding from the upper terrace to the lower one. Since the Mwanamakuka graves date back to the end of the 18th century this can also be used as evidence for the existence of a pre-18th century settlement in Bagamoyo.

b) Excavations

i) *Trenches Parallel to the Walls*

Trench 1 with its extensions was a long one after its completion, being of 1 x 30m. It was placed 2 m away and parallel to the south wall. The purpose of this trench was to find out if there were foundations of older rooms attached to the walls as suggested by window marks. The placing of the trench was such that any wall foundation radiating from the south wall would be crossed at about

2m from the wall. Since the trench was meant to cover the complete length of the south wall all older features attached or near the wall would be at least partially found.

The excavation interval was of 10 cm conducted carefully so that no feature was destroyed and that layers were not mixed. The first 20 centimetres were those of surface soil disturbed by recent cultivation of ground nuts, maize, beans and banana and partially by the land developer of the 1950s. It was after 30 cm that the accumulation of rubble neatly levelled began to appear with different concentrations. Since this also formed the floor of the brick house of the 1950s, this suggested that the levelling was done by the developer of that time period. Materials recovered from this level are those of modern time, including coins dating after 1940s (see Table 1).

Further down after 30 cm were discovered remains of walls and foundations of the older coral and rubble rooms (see Fig. 5). The thickness of the foundations which were 8 in total is 40cm. As the excavations cut through layers of soils to about 70cm, at the base of the foundations, three floors of occupation made of lime were observed on the section. At the bottom, an earlier one, probably not made of lime and coral, was also observed. The first, top floor, relates to the brick house construction and the next one down seems to relate to the well made lime floor which covered the whole courtyard attached to the storey house. It would seem that this courtyard floor had its counterpart in the rooms, suggesting a major renovation at that time of storey house building. The materials collected from between this floor and that of brick included coins dating after 1900.

The excavations in this trench also discovered posthole marks on both sides of the foundations suggesting that the roof of the houses had been supported not by the walls but by round wooden pillars (Fig.4). This would suggest that the houses were not roofed by concrete as in some Swahili buildings, but probably by metal sheeting or grass/palm fronds. Indeed not enough coral stones were observed in the lime-built foundations to support heavy roofing and that is another reason for using poles to support the roof.

The second floor of the coral and lime construction occurred between 40 and 50cm associated with German coins of 1890 to 1905 suggesting the German colonial period. In this floor were also found rings of semi-precious stones and beads. The next floor of coral and lime came after that, between 50 and 60 cm, which was also the end of the plastered walls. The plaster joined the floor neatly. No coin was found at this level. Below this last lime floor was found a simple floor of red soil suggesting an earlier simple house. No artifact was found on the red floor although concentration of soot and charcoal could be observed suggesting the use of fire.

It should be noted that the sequence above could not be observed from all sections of the trench except for the centre and south-east part. It would seem that the people occupying the site in the period of the storey house building converted some rooms on the west side of the southern wall into toilets. The trench in this area found pits which were made before the formation of the floor of the brick construction. The pits were covered by heavy metals including bars of railway lines which would easily suggest that the storey house and the toilets were built after 1891 when the Tanga railway line started being built and more so from 1900 when the Dar-es-Salaam line was being built (see Gwasa 1969; Brown 1970: 82-83).

To clarify the picture obtained from the long trench, one room was completely excavated (see book cover). The one selected had been found to have better pilaster preservation on the exposed walls and most floors appeared more clearly attached to this wall. Sections of different floors were left unexcavated with the intention of retaining it as a demonstration case as seen today on the site (Plate 2). The excavated room measured 3x3 m.

Trench 2 was placed parallel to the east wall. After establishing the knowledge of the existing sub-surface house structure in the south area, and indeed as it is preserved on the north wall, the same was assumed to have occurred all around the walls of caravan-serai. Excavations in Trench 1 had also found remains of a foundation suggesting extension of rooms to the east wall. Trench two was designated to track this foundation all the way to the north wall. The same method of excavation was used and more or less the same sequence of occupation was found. This side had 6 rooms, the largest measuring 8.5 x 4.5m and the smallest measuring 4.5 x 4m. The largest room could have been utilised as a storage facility. Actually the large rooms did not show much of lime floors suggesting that they were not used for living in.

Trench 3 on the west side also followed the inner foundation of the wall that had been discovered while excavating the south area. Some parts of the foundation at the centre had been demolished or did not exist (see Fig. 5). Also only two rooms could be observed in this area, one in the south corner and another in the north corner (Fig. 5). The central part of this side could have been disturbed by the post 1950 building of toilets, some of whose walls could be seen standing today (see Fig. 5).

The three long trenches described above uncovered pre-1950 house structures attached to the quadrangular walls of the caravan-serai. A total of 15 rooms were discovered, suggesting that together with the rooms still attached to the north wall there could have been more than 23 rooms. The excavations of Trenches 1 to 3 have also shown that different rooms could have been used for different functions as observed earlier.

ii) Trenches Inside the Storey House

Three trenches were sunk inside the storey house. One of 1x4m was placed in the north-west room, another of 1x4.5m with an extension of 1x1m was placed in the middle room and of 1x1m in the north-east narrow room (see Fig. 5). These are identical as Trenches 4, 5 and 6 respectively. The purpose of excavating inside the storey house was to see whether it was of the same age as the pre-1900 underground structures discovered in Trenches 1-3.

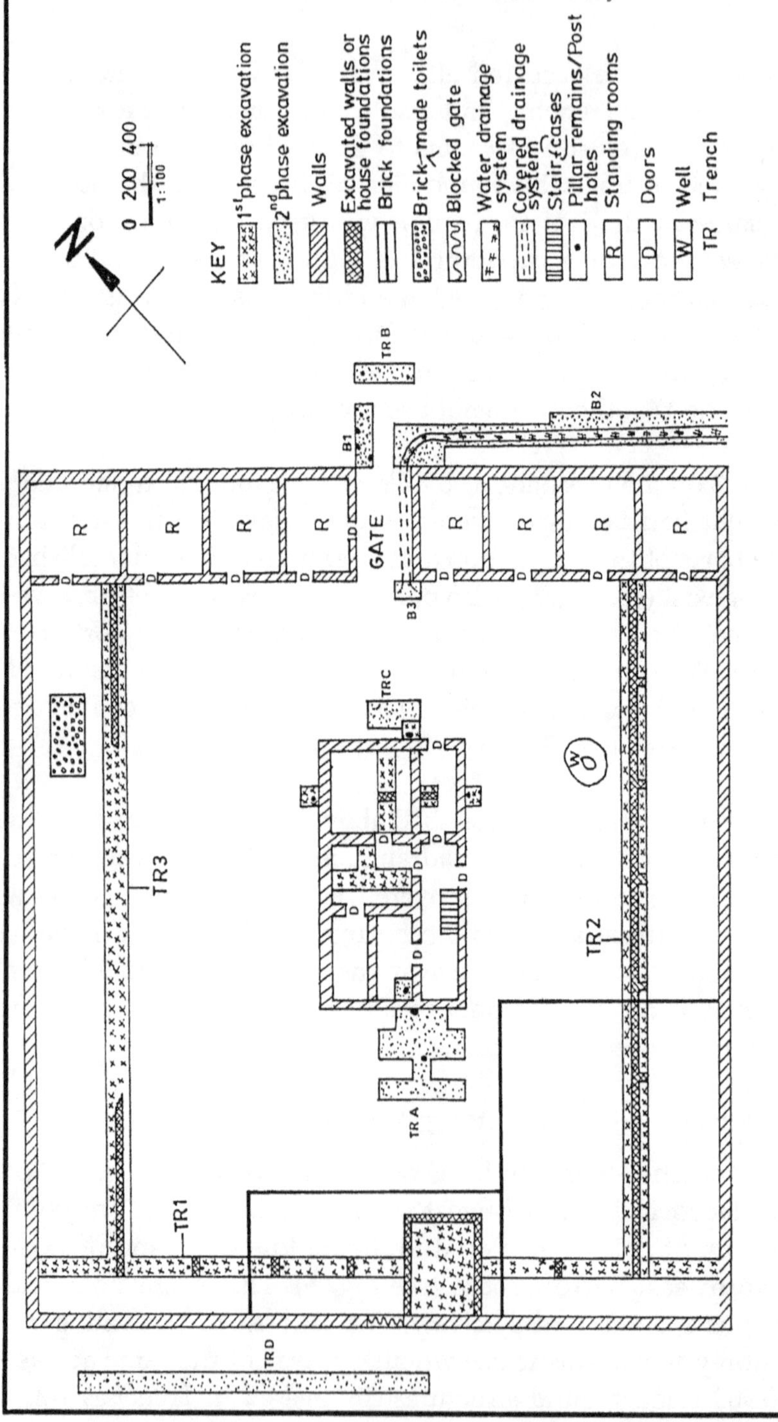
N
0 200 400
1:100
KEY
1st phase excavation
2nd phase excavation
Walls
Excavated walls or house foundations
Brick foundations
Brick made toilets
Blocked gate
Water drainage system
Covered drainage system
Stair cases
Pillar remains/Post holes
Standing rooms
Doors
Well
TR Trench
TR B
B1
B2
B3
GATE
R
D
TRC
W
TR3
TR2
TR A
TR1
TR D

Fig. 5: Caravan-serai site plan

Trench 4 had the first 20 cm made of the concrete floor of the storey house. After that a 10 cm layer of loose concrete materials mixed with sandy clay soils was crossed. It was after 30cm that an older foundation was exposed extending across the trench (see Fig. 5; Plate 2). The continuation of excavation also established a lime floor associated with the discovered foundation at about 40cm. However, the floor was not uniform: in some places it was thick and in others it was not visible at all. Excavations continued down to the sterile level at about 90-100cm were a sandy soil was reached. Artifacts recovered between 40 and 100cm were potsherds. Only two were decorated.

Trench 5, in the middle room, did not cross any earlier house foundation but exposed two layers of earlier floors below the modern house floor. Again these were not uniform in every place of the trench. It was shown earlier that two lime floors had been found in the outside trenches below the floor related to the storey house. The stratigraphy and material collected did not differ from those from the previous trenches. Trench 6 was aimed to find out if the wall foundation that had crossed Trench 4 had continued to the east side of the house. The excavation suggested that the wall had done so (see Fig. 5). Since the trench was also placed near the wall of the room, it was also found that this particular wall was less accurately built on a foundation of an earlier house foundation.

The first phase excavations ended up finding out if the older foundation discovered inside the storey house had extended outside the building. This was done assuming that the storey house foundation may not have been built on an older house plan. Three trenches, 7, 8, and 9 were sunk outside the walls where the earlier foundations were supposed to cross the storey house walls (see Fig. 5). What were found in each trench were remains of concrete pillars which suggested that the roof of the earlier existing house or structure was supported by them. This pattern was observed from rooms discovered in Trenches 1-2. The inventory of the material collected from phase one excavation is found in Table 1.

Examinations of the storey house wall foundations suggested that the house was not built on any earlier wall foundations. Since no wall foundation was found in Trench 5 it suggested that the place was less well built and probably there was a shelter in the middle of the courtyard. The older wall foundations discovered in Trench 4 and 6 could have supported such a shelter. When the storey house was built the sheltered area in the middle of the courtyard was removed to give way for the storey house.

PHASE TWO RESEARCH

The second phase research at caravan-serai had two main aims. First, to explore the main open space between the storey house and rooms discovered attached to the outer wall. As suggested earlier, this space is rectangular and although it was thought to be an open part of the courtyard it was necessary to show by excavations that it was the case. The second aim was to explore the general area outside the walls. Two hypotheses were to be tested. First, there could be other rooms attached or not attached to the walls providing services like toilets or servants quarters. Second, it was to examine the nature of the road or corridor that had been used to access the caravan-serai.

For the second point, oral traditions had asserted that there had been a main corridor running for a hundred metres from the then boundary of the town leading to the caravan-serai and so accessing it via its main gate. Caravan-serai was then built outside the town walls. Remains of the gate to the 100m corridor could be observed where the Top Life Bar is located today. As corollary to the second point, an observation during the first phase excavations of another gate, which was later filled in, suggested that there was a hind gate to the country side. Therefore, excavations on the front and hind site of the caravan-serai were planned. It was decided that trenches in phase 2 should be identified using letters (A, B,...) to contrast with numbers (1,2,...) of the first phase.

Trench A

The area between Trench 1 and the storey house was first examined. A long trench of 1 x 5m was sunk down to about 110cm. Only the last two layers of occupation were observed. Few artifacts were collected including local pottery, metal and glass beads. An extension of 1 x 1m towards the storey house was sunk to the same level. The only feature of interest observed was a pillar remains, found about 2.4m away from the wall of the storey house. This finding suggested that the earlier house structure/shelter found while excavating inside the house had its roof or canopy extending beyond the wall of the storey house on the southern side.

To prove that there had been a canopy another wide trench, an extension of A, was sunk towards the walls of 2.5 x 2m (see Plate 4). The floor associated with the storey house was broken. Below this was found a thin layer of soil of less than 5cm. This gave way to an earlier floor of lime of the occupation before the storey house was built. Four remains of pillars were found attached to the floor and continuing below it (see Plate 4). Three more pillars were found attached to the foundation of the storey house similar to those found earlier in the First Phase of excavations. The pillars found away from the wall of the house suggest that there had been a rectangular central house/structure roofed and with a canopy of about 1.5 m wide supported by a number of pillars whose remains are observed. Continued excavation, below the floor with the pillars, at about 30cm below the first floor, revealed a line of four other remains of pillars, not heavily built with lime, some being just postholes, about 1m from the wall. This suggested that the canopy had been narrower at the earlier phases of occupation and widened in the later phases. The examination of the wall foundation of the storey house at this area did not show any earlier foundation suggesting that the earlier simple structure was not built by lime but only supported by heavily built stone and lime pillars.

Trench B

This trench was sunk in front of the caravan-serai 4m away from the gate. It measured 1 x 3.5m across the main entrance. The main purpose of this trench was to see if there was any corridor made to enter the area. It was also made wide so as to find any wall remains that could have banked the corridor or series of pillars holding the fence that could have enclosed the corridor. The first 20cm were made of soil accumulated in the recent years. Between 20-30cm was found a layer of soils with some scattered rubble with no lime suggesting that it had been laid down probably by the builders of the storey house. It was between 30-35cm where a compact layer of lime and stones was reached extending 2m across the corridor suggesting that it was a road used to access the caravan-serai (Plate 5).

Below 35cm to 40cm was found a layer of soil with not many stones. In this layer was found a coin of 1880 suggesting that the well made road above it was post -1880. Below this soil to about 50cm was found another layer of compact materials with lime suggesting an earlier paved road of before 1880. From about 40cm, on both edges of the road, were observed marks of postholes (See Plate 5). The pillar marks suggest that there was a fence flanking the road/ corridor with a roof supported by pillars (Plate 5).

Another trench, designated B1, of 3 x 1 m, was sunk on the right side of the road near the gate as one enters the caravan-serai (Fig. 5). The purpose was to see if more postholes, reminiscent of those found in Trench B, had been lining the corridor. 3 such postholes were encountered at 40cm. Another Trench B2 was excavated one metre away from the wall on the left side of the gate. The objective of this trench was to find out if there had been a front canopy. Instead a water drainage furrow, more exposed by Trenches B2 (extension) and B3 (Fig. 5), was discovered. The materials collected from the bottom of the drainage furrow include coins of the1920s suggesting that it was built before that time. Excavations at Trench B3 further suggested that the furrow that had entered the caravan-serai along the eastern side of the gate had been covered by stones and lime probably to allow vehicles to be able to pass through the gate. This must have happened when the storey house had been built after 1900 has it is the same floor as that of the storey house that covered the furrow at the gate.

The opening of the furrow in the inner part of the gate reveal that the junction at which the furrow had branched east and west to collect water from all corners of the inside of the serai had been covered and blocked by concrete, metal bars and wires including vehicle springs. Whoever blocked the drainage system did not provide for an alternative. The older drainage system had at least two checkpoints where dirt was caught by prongs of iron rods built across the furrow: one such check-point was placed at the inner part of the gate and another one at the outer part. The tributaries (inside the serai) were narrower than the outlet (outside the serai). The opening of the Trench B3 also yielded a coin of 1891 from a thin soil layer occurring between the storey house floor (also covering the drainage) and the lower level that had been drained by the furrows. This finding strongly suggests that the drainage system had been serving the serai before the1890s and it was covered after that time. The finding was also proof beyond any doubt that the floor associated with the caravan-serai, and probably the house, was built after the 1890s, or more likely after 1990.

Trench C

This was sunk between the storey house and the main gate. It was of 1.5 x 3m being only 0.5 away from the north wall of the storey house. It was in this area near the wall foundation where earlier excavations (Trench 8) had found pillar remains, which would have supported the roof of the earlier structure. The picture obtained here corroborated what was observed in Trench A by observing four pillar structures attached to the lower floors suggesting that there had also been a canopy on this side of the house.

Trench D

This was sunk behind the caravan-serai being of 1 x 10m. This trench, which ran parallel to the wall of the caravan-serai, was placed 2m away from the wall. The purpose of this trench was to examine if the hind of the serai had been used for any function and also to find out if there had been a road through to the country, which had been blocked later.

The long trench had different stretches providing different patterns of stratigraphy. The large area of the middle part, where a narrow gate had been hypothesised to have existed, was found to have been used in the early phases of occupation as a hind exit as concentration of stones and lime occurred at about 60-80cm aligned to the hypothesised gate. This earliest phase of occupation does not show many artifacts suggesting that there was not much activity in the area behind the caravan-serai. In the later period the hind of the caravan-serai was used as a dumping place. Between 20 and 60 cm were found a pile of mixed-up materials including local and imported ceramics, many metal objects including bullets and their shells, glass, beads and rubble. The greatest concentration was near the blocked gate suggesting that the dwellers did not go far from the gate to dump garbage. The piling and the accumulation of materials stopped only after the gate had been covered, probably by the storey house builders after 1900. Probably the role of the place as caravan-serai had changed and only a few people lived in the place then.

The examination of stratigraphy of the long trench further away from the dump towards west, also suggested the existence of toilets used at the later period, but before the gate was blocked. The break and the down sloping of the layer of lime and rubble observed at 40 cm, and indeed the observation of dark layer of soil near the bottom of the trench representing toilet remains suggested that the place had been used as a toilet. It was not possible to find out if the hind area had been used as toilets from the beginning of occupation as more excavations in the area were required to check the hypothesis. Indeed, after the hind gate had been blocked toilets were built inside as shown in Trench 1.

Trench E

This was the last trench in phase two and it was sunk inside the storey house (Fig. 4) to check if the southern wall of the storey house had been built on an earlier house foundation. This trench was a further attempt to prove that the middle of the caravan-serai was less built before the storey house. The concrete remains of a pillar like those observed elsewhere was found below the house floor and there was no foundation of an earlier structure.

Plate 1(a): Front view of caravan-serai

Plate 1(b): Caravan-serai as seen from inside

Plate 2: The room opened at Trench 1 showing occupation floors.

Plate 3: Earlier house/structure's foundation below the floor of the storey house.

Plate 4: Pillar remains from Trench 4.

Plate 5: Corridor trench (B) showing road layers.

Plate 6: Imported ceramics.

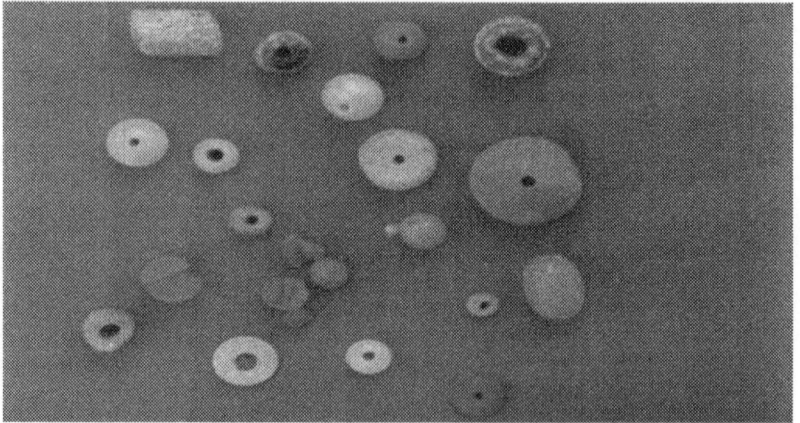

Plate 7: Glass beads.

Plate 8: Some of the German coins found in Trench B and D.

(a)

(b)

Plate 9: Mwanamakuka tombs and the Fort respectively.

CHAPTER 8

MATERIALS COLLECTED

The total material collection of the two phases of excavation is shown in Tables 1-4. Since the purpose of this work is not to describe each artifact, the presentation below is according to arbitrary classes established from the materials recovered from the excavations. 2 general classes recognised here as non-metallic and metallic materials are used to simplify the presentation of the materials. In the non-metallic category we have 12 sub-classes including ceramics, beads, glass and bones of animals and shells. In the metallic category 13 sub-classes have been recognised, including nails, screw/nuts/bolts, coins and rings.

NON-METALLIC

CERAMICS

A total of 2869 local ceramics were collected from all phases of excavations. Most of this sub-class of pottery seems to have been small pots with short necks and some carination or a dependent restricted vessel (Fig. 6a-b). These are pottery dated from between AD 1700-1900. Those found from the early floors of occupation seem to be of what has been termed elsewhere as post-post Swahili ware found in good number on the central and southern coast of Tanzania in settlements associated with the rise of the new phase of the Swahili towns after the Omani takeover of the coast of East Africa from about 1700-1890.

Another sub-class of local pottery is the one collected mostly from the midden behind the caravan-serai. This is a type of pottery rare on the coast and so far this tradition has only been found in the area of the Bagamoyo caravan-serai. This pottery, with bands of oblique incisions sometimes appearing separately or associated with pendant triangles and sometimes with bands of oblique comb stamping (Fig.6c-e), is also found in the deep interior including south-western Tanzania (Mapunda-pers. Com.), as well as in the Great Lakes Region by the recent University of Dar-es-Salaam Field School and described as pottery of post AD 1700 (Kwekason and Chami 2003). Soper and Golden (1969) found the same pottery still in use in Mwanza (see their Plate XI:1-7) and therefore attributed it to the Sukuma people. This pottery seems to have arrived in the Bagamoyo area through the central trade route associated with the ivory and slave trade.

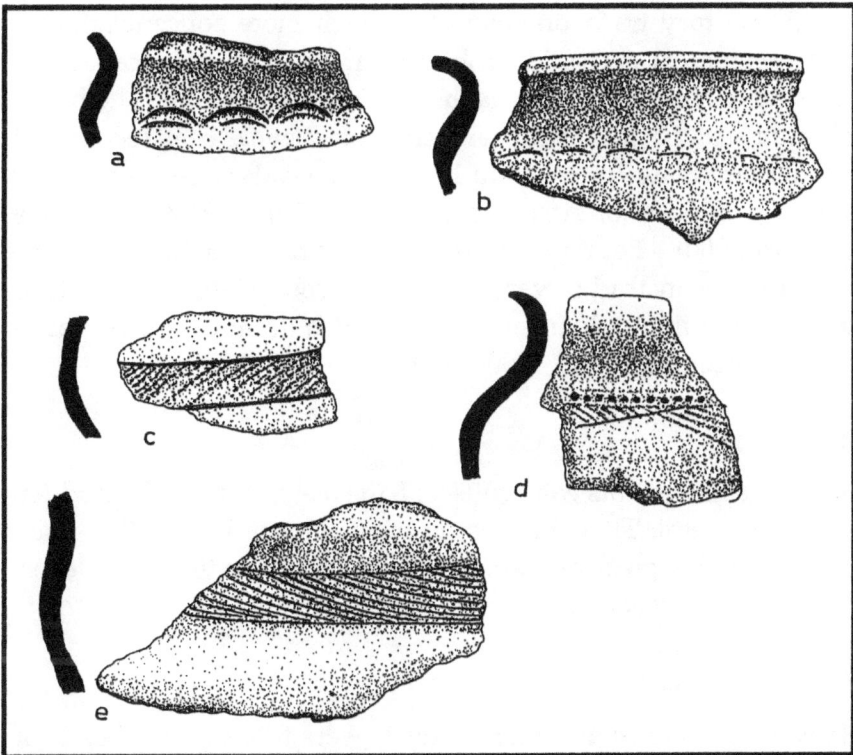

Fig. 6: Local ceramics from caravan-serai (*a* and *b* are of the 19th century coastal tradition and *c* to *e* are of the 17th to 19th century western Tanzanian tradition.

Imported Ceramics

A total of 466 pieces were recovered mainly from the midden behind the caravan-serai. The first category is the Chinese and European porcelain (Plate 6). The second category is the unglazed thin pottery of reddish-pink fabric with decorating lines of black paint (Plate 6). The origin of this pottery is probably India (Chittick 1984). This pottery is again associated with the slave period as it was also found by this author in caves associated with slave trade in Mwangapwani, north of Zanzibar.

BEADS

Surprisingly only 50 beads were recovered from all phases of excavations. Since beads were one of the significant items during the 19th century trade one expected much more concentration at the caravan-serai. As has been observed from all coastal excavations, beads have rivalled pottery as the most numerous find. The beads collected are all of late European period of what has been recognised as Venetian (Plate 7; see Dubin 1987). Such beads were spread over many other parts of Africa in the 18th and the 19th century (see Kinahan 2000). Four red barrel beads with black inside, of the early European trade, were also recovered (Plate 7). This find suggests that the trade in such beads which dominated the coastal trade between 1550 and 1700 had declined by then.

GLASS

Many glass fragments were collected, the majority from the midden behind the serai. They all seem to have belonged to bottles. Only one identifiable piece of glass was recovered from the lower levels of Trench 1: it was a bottle from New York with a date of 1875.

BONES AND SHELLS

Many animal bones and marine shells were found. Most bones of the animals seem to belong to cattle and ovicaprids suggesting that they are remains of food. Since the shells appear not in piles these may have been brought to the serai for purposes other than food.

METALS

The metal category had the largest amount of artifacts collected. This category includes nails and screws, coins, bullet and bullet shells, chains and earrings.

NAILS/SCREWS

This is the largest find probably due to the use of nails and screws in house construction of all periods. This activity left many of them scattered all over the place. 1583 nails and screws were collected (Table 1&4).

COINS

Coins are an important category of our findings because they are also used as a chronometric method. Where they are found in an undisturbed context, the layer they are found in and the associated materials are of the same date as the coin or thereafter (*terminus post quem*) (Renfrew and Bahn 1991: 125). Several coins were recovered from different contexts some being *in situ*. The collection include those of the Sultan of Zanzibar (1880), the Germans and those of the British (post 1900). 21 coins were collected (Plate 8).

BULLETS AND SHELLS

One complete bullet, yet unfired, and 8 shells were recovered. The examination of these by a police officer at Bagamoyo suggested that they were those used by early rifles.

Table 1: *Materials collected from Phase One excavations.*

T	Dth	Non-Metalic								Metalic				
		Lce	Ice	Be	Gl	Bu	Bn	Sh	Sp	N/b	Co	Ri	Ch	Bu/sh
1	30-85	1108	272	18	327		306	369	1	1087	7	1	1	7
2	30-95	76	10	9	4	5	40	3		67				
3	30-80	52	10		12		26	2		15	1			
4	30-90	14						3						
5	30-50	6						1		27				
Total		1256	292	27	343	5	372	378	1	1196	8	1	1	7

T=trench, Dth=depth, Lce=local ceramics, Ice=imported ceramics, Be=beads, Gl=glass, Bu=button, Bn=bone, Sh=shells, Sp=spindle, N/b=nails/bolts, Co=coins, Ri=rings, Ch-chain, Bu/sh=bullet/shells.

Table 2: *Non-metallic materials collected from Trench A.*

T	Dth	Lce	Ice	Be	Gl	Bu	Ru	Pl	Ny	mn	Bn	Sh	Cn	Gr
A/i	40-79	30	3								14	4		
	70-80	27										4		
	80-90				1						1			
	90-100	1			1							1		1
	100-110						1							
A/ii	0-30	3			20		3	1		4	49	11		
	30-40	1									1	2		
	40-50				1						1	3		
	50-60	5						1			1	1		
A/ii/a	20-30	2												
	30-40	4												
	40-50							1						
A/ii/b	20-30	12			8						20	8		
	30-40	14						1			3	2		
A/ii/c	0-20										4			
	20-30													
	30-40	1			1						1	1		
	40-50										1	1		
TOTAL		100	3	0	32	0	4	4	0	4	95	38	0	1

Abbreviations are as in Table 1. For this table: Mn=manila, Pl=plastic, Ru=rubber, Cn=coconut and Gr=graphite.

Table 3: *Non-metallic materials recovered from Trenches B-D.*
 (Abbreviations are as in Tables 1 & 2).

T	Dth	Lce	Ice	Be	Gl	Bu	Ru	Pl	Ny	Mn	Bn	Sh	Cn	Gr
B	0-20	10			33			10			22	28		
	20-30	9			9			4			22	28		
	30-40	9		2	5						33	20		
	40-50	8			4						21	32		
	50-60	5									2	3		
	60-70	19			1									
	70-80	4	4											
	80-90	1		1										
	90-100	1										2		
B/i	40-50		3	1	3						6	16		
	50-60	5			1						1	21		
B/ii	10-20	23			30			6			41	21		
	20-30	19	19	1	79			5			35	49		
	30-40	8	15		36			14			56	110		
	40-50	8	3		10			13			27	69		
	50-60	2	2	1	17							13		
C	0-20											3		
	20-30											5		
	40-50	1												
	50-60	11												
D	0-30	417	9	20	88			2			217	80		
	30-40	209	14	5	24					1	96	51		
	40-50	352	95	14	175	1		1			228	155		
	50-60	9	2		7						18	19		
	60-70	57		3	23	3					70	88	1	
	70-80	16	2								14	10		
	80-90	3					1		1		4	7		
Total		1206	168	21	545	4	1	55	2		913	787	1	

Table 4: *Metallic materials collected from the second phase excavations.*

T	Dth	N/b	Kn	Nd	Lc	Bu/sh	Ri	Er	Co	Tn	Al	Bt
A/i	40-70	2			5							
	70-80	1										
A/ii	0-30	9									3	
A/ii/a	20-30	1										
	40-50	14										
	50-60	1										
B	0-20	9							2			
	20-30	9				1			1			1
	30-40								1			
	40-50								1			
	50-60	1										
B/i	10-20	24							1	6		
	20-30	24					1	1	1	32		
B/ii	30-40	15					4			41		
	40-50	6								14		
	50-60								1			
D	0-30	49	3	2	1		3		2			5
	30-40	36										
	40-50	76							2		1	
	50-60	4				1						3
	60-70	23										3
	70-80	3										
TOTAL		307	3	2	1	2	8	1	12	93	4	12

Table 4: Metallic materials collected from the second phase excavations. Some abbreviations are as in Table 1. For this table, Kn=Knife, Nd=Needle, Lc=lock, Er=earring, Tn=tin, Al=aluminium, Bt=Batteries.

N.B. Some of the abbreviations are as in Table 1. For this table, Kn=Knife, Nd=Needle, Lc=lock, Er=earring, Tn=tin, Al=aluminium, Bt=Batteries.

CHAPTER 9

SOME GENERAL DISCUSSION

This discussion involves issues of interest that led to the excavation of the Bagamoyo caravan-serai. The issues include: the beginning of caravan-serai in relation to the rise of Bagamoyo; the historical development of caravan-serai; the function of caravan-serai as a location in Bagamoyo; the role played by caravan-serai in the wider international trade involving mainly ivory and slaves; and lastly methodological lessons.

THE BEGINNING OF CARAVAN-SERAI

Probably the most comprehensive publication about the origin of Bagamoyo so far is that of Brown (1970). Caravan-serai does not seem to have appeared in the early history of Bagamoyo traced at the graves of Mwanamakuka to the end of the 18th century. It was shown that the earliest caravan-serai could have been built in the 1870s. This could have been the same place mentioned in the 1860s as Shamba Gonera belonging to one Maghram although the place was located far from town. This is probably the same person who could have changed his farm into a caravan-serai. The construction could have taken several years, the dream being realised only in the 1970s.

It was shown that the earliest paved road to the area was that made before 1880, and since the layer in which the coin is found is a thin one of five centimetres, this would suggest that the place was not built many years before the layer with the coin. Any earlier occupation before the first road layer would have been of a simpler settlement probably of a farmer who would have sold the land to

Maghram. The beginning of the Bagamoyo caravan-serai as a functioning lodge can therefore be placed between 1870-1875, and any existence of it before that date was a mere farm or a site under construction. A date before 1870 makes historical mention of the farm "Shamba Gonera" in that general area, and a date of 1875 occurs in the map of Bagamoyo (Fig. 3). Excavations have provided a layer of coral and lime for the road to the area of before 1880.

This conclusion has a major implication for the role Bagamoyo played in the coastal-interior trade before 1870. It will be shown later that the date between 1840, when Seyyid Said established Zanzibar as his capital, and 1870 when we see caravan-serai being built, was the time when trade to the interior and exploration of Africa is being encouraged from Zanzibar. The late building of caravan-serai at Bagamoyo, 30 years after the Oman Sultan had made Zanzibar his capital, suggests that Bagamoyo was still competing with some other localities such as Kaole, Kunduchi, Dar-es-Salaam and Saadani-Pangani for economic supremacy. Indeed, to reiterate this point, several historical records suggest that Bagamoyo was not the only place used as a passage to and from the interior. The trip by Burton and Speke of 1857 did not utilise Bagamoyo, but Kaole (Simpson 1975). It was only after 1870 that most caravans utilised Bagamoyo and hence the building of the caravan-serai. It would also seem that there was a Barracks at Kaole, also used to offer the services of caravan-serai. This place was referred to as a Baluchi Barracks used by Burton and Speke to recruit potters and guides. It has been noted earlier that more than two hundred Baluchis were involved.

A second example is the failed attempt of Sultan Majid, the successor of Seyyid Said in 1860, to build Mzizima, which he called Dar-es-Salaam, as his new capital away from Zanzibar. It was in Dar-es-Salaam where Tippu Tip was summoned by Majid in 1866 from the deep interior to account for the interior trade. If that project had been carried forward by his brother, successor Said Baragash, after 1872, the Dar-es-Salaam, and not Bagamoyo, would have become the most important entrepot. It seems that because Baragash neglected Dar-es-Salaam Bagamoyo was promoted by him using people such as Maghram who also expanded the simple house near the beach to become a castle which would serve the Sultan's interests (Plate 9).

A third example is the decision by the French Catholic missionaries to build their evangelising centre at Bagamoyo. In thinking about where to put the centre in the 1860s the options oscillated between Dar-es-Salaam, Bagamoyo and Saadani-Pangani. This suggested that there was no single well established place on the central coast of Tanzania where one was forced by circumstances, such as a King's residence or main port, to build an evangelising centre. The choice of Bagamoyo came about because land was available and probably due to the reason that it was closer to Zanzibar. The building of the missionary centre itself contributed to the rise of Bagamoyo because European traders and travellers would have started using it due to the facilities there.

THE ROLE OF CARAVAN-SERAI

The construction of caravan-serai took place, therefore, at the time when Bagamoyo was thought to be an unrivalled entrepot on the coast of East Africa from about 1870. By then the town had been settled by Swahili and Asiatic traders who were building residential and trade houses including warehouses (also see Brown 1970). As virtually all the caravan trade and exploration trips from Zanzibar were now directed to pass through Bagamoyo, there was a great need for a facility like caravan-serai to be built.

As noted earlier in chapter 1 caravan-serai is a kind of inn in eastern countries. According to The Encyclopedia Americana, the root of the word is *caravan* which is a Persian word used "to denote large companies which travel together in Asia and Africa for the sake of security from robbers, having in view, principally, trade or pilgrimages." A caravan-serai is a place where caravans put up. It is supposed to be a large quadrangular building, enclosing a spacious courtyard, small rooms constituting the interior. Another character of the caravan-serai is a large gateway used as the entrance. The excavations reported in this work have shown that Bagamoyo caravan-serai had all these characteristics.

Although serai acted as inns, they were not furnished and the traveller had to supply his own needs. Caravan-serai were built by pious Mohammedans to provide a resting place for travellers and not for business. Only in a few cases were persons kept in the place to guide the caravans for some distance. It is not certain now whether the Bagamoyo caravan-serai was used for business or as a place of rest without payment before people continued with their journey. It is not even certain whether there were persons stationed there to run the facility and guide travellers for a distance. A report by Burton and Speke suggested that a similar facility at Kaole, probably more modest, recorded as a garrison, had Baluchi Soldiers who were also used to guide travellers for a distance during the trip to the interior (Simpson 1975).

The building of the Bagamoyo caravan-serai by one rich and probably pious Maghram, in his 'Shamba Gonera', slightly outside the then Bagamoyo town, was probably not meant for business. There is no evidence from the excavations that there were trading activities going on in the Bagamoyo caravan-serai. If there had been any then there would have remained a reasonable amount of prominent trade goods of the time such as beads and valuable ceramics. Also, the small amount of local ceramics suggests that only few, if any, people resided in the caravan area.

It would seem, therefore, the main role of the caravan-serai was to offer sanctuary to the individuals involved in the caravan trade. The evidence available suggests that it was a typical inn described earlier, where those who were calling in would have had carried or brought in supplies for their own needs. Again it is not reported if the established Zanzibar traders, i.e. Tippu Tip or the European explorers, did stay in the caravan-serai. With the presence of hotels which could have been built in the town by then such prominent people could have avoided a self-service caravan-serai. Records show that there existed a hotel along the Indian Street which would probably have catered for such people.

Although Stanley (1878) does not say where he himself stayed, he talked about a number of his caravan crew, Zanzibaris and Nyamwezis, getting out of their camp and entering the town where they created havoc by stealing and raping. It is not clear whether the camp was another name for caravan-serai, or whether there was another camp-like place where a class of caravan crew stayed. The map of 1875 shows that there existed a slave camp near the caravan-serai. Whether this is the same camp reported by Stanley is not clear.

The building of caravan-serai at Bagamoyo also played the role of enticing traders to pass through the town due to the existence of such a service. This guaranteed the economic growth of the town because, due to those facilities, traders spent money in Bagamoyo through trade and other social services. The bulk of the caravan crew staying in Bagamoyo waiting to be recruited and indeed the amount of slaves kept in Bagamoyo awaiting to be sold or transported to Zanzibar increased demand for social and other economic services. No wonder that the choice by the Deutsch Oest Africa, a German Company, to make Bagamoyo the capital of its East Africa Company emanated from the fact that facilities for various administrative activities existed in the town of Bagamoyo by 1880s.

CULTURAL PROCESSES AT THE BAGAMOYO CARAVAN-SERAI

FIRST PHASE

It was noted that before 1870 the area of the caravan-serai could have had simple mud/wattle structures. Whether these belonged to the individual(s) who sold this land to the caravan-serai builder or to the builder himself is not known. The evidence for this occupation was uncovered in the excavation of one room attached to the southern wall and found at the lowest layer with dark spots, charcoal fr gments and red soils used in the house plastering process. This layer was found after breaking the earliest lime floor associated with the first occupation of coral and lime. Also other trenches yielded cultural materials such as pottery below the lowest lime floors or pavements.

SECOND PHASE

This phase is that of 1870-1880 being that of the first occupation of the stone-built caravan-serai. This must have been during the heyday of the Bagamoyo ivory and slave trade, the period when the town became the unrivalled entrepot of the mainland coast of East Africa, opening the Indian Ocean to the heart of the African continent. It should be noted that this is the time when Zanzibar was used as a starting point to explore Africa via Bagamoyo and virtually all the exploration expeditions then passed through here. It will be recalled that this was after the time when Speke and Grant had managed to pass through Bagamoyo, successfully ending up in Cairo, which stimulated further explorations leading to the travels of Stanley and Cameron.

In the records of Tippu Tip we also read of the intensification of the caravan trade to Uganda (Farrant 1975), Congo and the rest of central Africa at this time. The Swahili traders had full control of the interior Kingdoms and as they were answerable to Zanzibar, Bagamoyo became the main gate to the heart of Africa. As reported in Tippu Tip's reports, virtually all caravans between 1870-1890 passed via Bagamoyo (Farrant 1975).

It would seem that something happened between the few years before 1880 and after, probably before 1884. The indication of this is the accumulation of a thin layer of soil between the earlier floor and the subsequent one observed over a number of places excavated. This was more obvious in the open room and the entrance road to the caravan-serai where the sole coin of 1880 was found below the second lime floor. This suggests that there was a refurbishment of the caravan-serai area some time after 1880. The refurbishment may have come about after the German takeover and after the clamping down of the slave trade in the late 1970s and early 1880s (Farrant 1975). The total abolition of slave trade occurred in 1876. Since the slave trade contributed much to the caravan trade, as slaves were also carriers of other commodities, there is no question that few if any slave caravans would have come to Bagamoyo after 1876. Tippu Tip himself, as found by the Europeans after 1880, continued transporting slaves to the coast but in the guise of free porters. Tippu Tip could have done that only because he was a powerful man, not only feared by Europeans, but also needed for security and peace along the caravan route and in the whole of western Tanzania and central Africa.

THE THIRD PHASE

This is of 1880-1891 which coincided with the European activities in the town of Bagamoyo and elsewhere. The later part of this period from 1887 is also the time when colonialism was declared and Bagamoyo became the capital of colonial Germany in Tanzania. Trade was mainly based on other items apart from slaves who were now brought to Bagamoyo through unofficial routes and sometimes in the guise of porters. From 1886 the Germans organised their own trade expeditions to the interior which infuriated the Bagamoyo rulers who had failed to make the Germans pay tribute to them. The new era is shown at the caravan-serai by the new well made floor all over the serai and the corridor. Below it is the coin of the 1880 discussed earlier and above this floor is another coin of 1891. The coin of 1891, as mentioned earlier, was found in a completely thin and sealed layer between the floor of 1880s and the last one laid down sometime after 1891 (the date of the coin) which was used also to cover the original drainage system described earlier. The post-1891 floor is also the one associated with the storey house at the middle of Caravan-Serai. The coin of 1891 was found while opening the inlet of the drainage furrow at the inner part of the main gate.

The amount of coins found for this time period suggest that trade flourished at Bagamoyo even after the slave trade had faded away and after the Abushiri war. Most coins belonged to Deutch Oest Africa suggesting the new economic power in the region. Even when the Germans moved capital from Bagamoyo to Dar-es-Salaam in 1891 trade activities continued unabated at Bagamoyo. Caravan-serai has more coins dating between 1892-1905 than any other period. Of course the region experienced a dramatic growth of the economy during the European colonial period and even when Bagamoyo had ceased being the capital it would still have experienced relatively more economic activities than before (see Brown 1970: 82-83).

THE FOURTH PHASE

This begins arbitrarily after 1905 to 1950. It would seem that Bagamoyo had gone down economically and the caravan-serai was no longer serving caravans.

Archaeologically it would seem that the caravan-serai got a new face-lift by having a structure/shelter existing in the courtyard demolished and a modern storey house built in its place. The central structure may have probably been non-existent for a number of years or decades as the foundation of it was found 20 cm below the floor of the storey house. This storey house, which has been described before, had its floor extended outside to cover the open courtyard and touching the rooms attached to the quadrangular walls (Plate 1). This floor was not however extended inside the rooms, suggesting that the new developer had no residential purpose for those rooms, apart from those on the northeast side. He/she actually went ahead and converted some of those to the south into toilets using railway metal to cover the pits. He/she probably did this after blocking the gate used as an exit to the toilets on the south wall. He/she also blocked the windows of all the rooms except those on the north wall. This developer also covered the drainage system which collected water from inside the caravan-serai by his new floor. At the gate, the deep drainage system was covered by the use of car-springs and wire mesh was used to support lime mortar. It would seem that the purpose of doing this was to increase security and to enable him/her to bring vehicles/horse carts inside the caravan-serai. This also suggests that the role of the caravan-serai as a guest house had stopped and the rooms were used rather as stores, this being the reason for blocking the windows.

The storey house seems to have been built between 1905-1920 as the only datable materials found above its associated floor are British coins dating after 1900. The non-utilisation and failure to repair rooms attached to the walls led to their deterioration and probable collapse thereafter.

THE FIFTH PHASE

This dates after the 1950s to the present when the monument was refurbished. The developer of the 1950s, who seems, to have stored bulky things in the area, levelled the larger part of the caravan-serai apart from the rooms of the north wall. On this new floor and that associated with the storey house he built his cement brick rooms attached to the outer walls. He/she did not utilise the foundations of the earlier rooms he had levelled. It was from this time the caravan-serai adopted the form of today, more so after the collapse of the rooms made of bricks. It would also seem that the brick-house builder moved the toilets to the west wall near the northern corner.

A MODEL FOR THE ANCIENT TRADE

It should be noted that this is probably the first known caravan-serai excavated on the coast of East Africa. It is likely that similar caravan-serai existed elsewhere on the coast in the past but not recorded or their structure confused with other types of buildings. It is known today that a trading emporium visited by foreign traders existed from years before BC/AD changeover. The best reported is that of Rhapta at the time of the Graeco-Romans followed by that of Kilwa between AD1200-1500. The archaeology of the ancient coastal civilisations concentrated on showing that East Africa was more oriented towards the ocean rather than the interior. However, recent works have paid attention to the coastal-interior connections showing that trade routes penetrating deep into Africa existed before the 19th century AD. In the absence of written records and the dearth of trade goods excavated it has been difficult to demonstrate the routes and the actual trade goods.

One aspect which has been proposed, however, is that alignment of sites of the same time period, and more so of similar cultural periods, from the coast to the deep interior of Africa could be used to suggest cultural trade contact (Chami 1994). This model was used to dispute the idea that such a spread of archaeological sites reflected people's migration. For instance, it had been argued that the spread of the Early Iron Working sites from the Great Lakes Region to the coast reflected the immigration of Bantu speakers to the coast. Prof. Chami has argued to the contrary that such a spread reflected the spread of a tradition through regular contact probably made feasible through a regular trade route. The evidence used for that hypothesis was the ancient documents of Graeco-Roman times suggesting that such trading towns existed and that at least one Roman traveller followed a route to the Great Lakes Region. The find of Roman trade goods at the coast also suggested that similar materials could be found in the interior.

Also excavations of sites dating between AD 600-900 radiating from Bagamoyo area to as far as Morogoro with trade goods found as far as 40km from the coast suggest a similar hypothesis (Chami 1994; Håland and Msuya 2000). The excavation at caravan-serai has provided the first incontrovertible data to corroborate the model. It was discussed earlier that pottery similar to that found in western Tanzania in about the 19th century has been recovered from the Bagamoyo caravan-serai. This is the first find of its kind on the coast of East Africa, suggesting that trade between Bagamoyo and its deep hinterland spread a tradition of pottery established in the deep interior of Africa to the coast. The fact that this has only been identified at Bagamoyo would support the idea that the tradition followed the trade route. From Bagamoyo the route branched at Tabora leading to the different parts of the lake regions and to Zambia and Congo. The portery was probably brought to the coast by porters some of whom were Nyamwezi. It is known that some of the Nyamwezi traders and porters settled in the region of Bagamoyo.

One question which would arise from this conclusion is why the 19th century tradition has not been found elsewhere on the coast when compared with those of the earlier tradition particularly that of the EIW people. This is probably due to the short-lived long-distance trade between the deep interior and the coast. Whereas the EIW tradition lasted more than 4 centuries, we see the 19th century trade lasting for less than a century. Probably more time was needed for the interior traditions to be spread to other parts of the coast.

REFERENCES

Alpers, E. (1969)
"The Coast and the Development of the Caravan Trade." in kimambo and Temu, J. (eds) *A History of Tanzania*. Dar es Salaam, Historical association of Tanzania, p. 35-56.

Areskough, A. and Persson, H. (1999)
In the Heart of Bagamoyo: The Decoding of a Coastal Town in Tanzania. Lund: Lund University.

Brown, W.T. (1970)
"Bagamoyo: An Historical Introduction." *Tanzania Notes and Records* 71: 69-84.

Burton, R. 1872
Zanzibar: City, Island and Coast. London: Tinsley Brothers.

Chami, F. A. (1990)
"Changwehela: A Submerged Slave Town South of Bagamoyo." In Sinclair, P. and G. Pwiti (Eds), *Urban Origins in Eastern Africa: Proceedings of a 1990 workshop Harare and Great Zimbabwe*, p. 124-8. Stockholm: The Swedish Central Board.

Chami, F. A. (1992a)
"Current Archaeological Research in the Bagamoyo District, Tanzania." In Sinclair, P and A. Juma (Eds), *Urban Origin in Eastern Africa: Proceedings of the 1991 workshop in Zanzibar*, p.15-35. Stockholm: The Swedish Central Board.

Chami, F.A. (1992b)
"Early Urban Settlements: A Conceptual Problem." Paper read at the World Archaeological Congress, Mombasa.

Chami, F.A. (1994)
Tanzanian Coast in the First Millenium AD. Studies in African Archaeology, 7. Uppsala: Societas Archeologica Uppsaliensis.

Chami, F. A. (1998)
"A Review of Swahili Archaeology." *African Archaeological Review*, 5(3): 199:218.

Chami F.A. (2001)
"The Archaeology of the Rufiji basin Since 1987-2000." in Chami F.A.; Pwiti G. & Radimilahy, C. (eds), *People Contacts and the Environment in the African Past*. Studies in the African Past 1, Dar e salaam, Dar es Salaam University Press Ltd.

Chami F.A. (2002a)
"The Swahili World." in Chami, F.A. and Pwiti, G. (eds): *Southern Africa and the Swahili World*. Dar e salaam, Dar es Salaam University Press Ltd. p. 1-14.

Chami, F.A. (2002b)
"The Excavations of Kaole Ruins." In Chami, F. and Pwiti, G. (eds), *Southern Africa and the Swahili World.* Studies in the African Past 2. Dar es Salaam, Dar-es-Salaam University Press p. 25-49.

Chittick, N. (1962)
"Recent Discoveries in Tanganyika." Actes du VI Congrës Panafricain de Prëhistoire et de l'ëtude du Quaternaire. Turvuren: *Musee Royal de l'Afrique Centrale* 3: 215-23.

Chittick, N. (1970)
"Relics of the Past in the Region of Dar-es-Salaam." *Tanzania Notes and Records* 71:65-68

Chittick, N. (1974)
Kilwa: An Islamic Trading Cty on the East African Coast (2vols): *The Finds.* Nairobi: BIEA.

Chittick, N. (1984)
Manda: Excavations at an Island Port on the Kenya Coast. Nairobi: British Institute in Eastern Africa.

Connah, G. (1996)
Kibiro: The Salt of Bunyoro: Past and Present. London: BIEA.

Datoo, B.A. (1975)
Port Development in East Africa: Dar-es-Salaam. East Africa Literature Bureau.

Dubin, L. (1987)
The History of Beads: From 3,000 BC to the Present. London, Thames and Hudson.

Gray, Sir. J.M. (1957)
"Trading Expeditions From the Coast to Lakes Tanganyika and Victoria Before 1857." *Tanganyika Notes and Records* 49: 226-46.

Farrant, L. (1975)
Tippu Tip and the East African Slave Trade. London Hamish Hamilton.

Gwasa, G. (1969)
"The German intervention and African resistance in Tanzania." In Kimambo, I. and Temu, J. (eds). *A History of Tanzania.* Dar-es-Salaam: Historical Association of Tanzania, p. 85-122.

Hålland, R. and Msuya, C. (2000)
"Pottery Production, Iron Working and Trade in the EIA: The Case of Dakawa, East-central Tanzania." *Azania* 35: 2000.

Henschel, J. (2000)
Listen to the Story of the Tombs: Bagamoyo Mission 1870-1930. Peramiho: Peramiho Printing Press.

Hirth, K. (1978)
"Interregional Trade and the Formation of Prehistoric Gateway Communities." *American Antiquity* 43(1): 35-45.

Hodges, R. (1982)
    Dark Age Economics. London: Durkworth.
Hodges, R. (1988)
    Primitive and Peasant Markets. Oxford: Basil Blackwell.
Iliffe, J. (1969)
    Tanganyika Under German Rule 1905-1912. Cambridge: University Press.
Kinahan, J. (2000)
    Cattle for Beads: The Archaeology of Historical Contact and Trade on the Namibia Coast. Studies in the African Archaeology 17. Uppsala: Actas Archaeological Uppsaliensis
Kwekason, A. (2002)
    "Geo-environmental Aspects of the Dar-es-Salaam Area." In Chami, F, and Pwiti, G. (eds), *Southern Africa and the Swahili World*, 15-24. Studies in the African Past 2. Dar-es-Salaam: University Press.
Kwekason A. and Chami, F. (2003)
    "The Archaeology of Muleba, South West of Lake Nyanza: A Preliminary Report." In Chami, F., Pwiti, G. and Radimilahy, C. (eds). *Climate Change, Trade and Modes of Production in the Sub-Saharan Africa*. Studies in the African Past 3. Dar-es-Salaam: Dra es Salaam University PressLtd.
Kusimba, C. (1999)
    The Rise and Fall of Swahili States. London: AltaMira Press.
Morgan, W. (1973)
    East Africa. London: Longman.
Nurse, D and T. Spear (1985)
    The Swahili. Philadelphia:University of Pennsylvania Press.
Pikirayi, I. (2003)
    "Shifiting Patterns of Trade in the Western Indian Ocean Zone - Northern Zimbabwe: 1500-1750 AD." in Chami F.A. pwiti, G. and Radimilahy, C. (eds): *Climate Change, Trade and Modes of Production in Sub-Saharan Africa*. Dar es Salaam, dar es Salaam University Press Ltd. p. 129-154.
Posnansky, M. (1975)
    "Connections Between the Lacustrine Peoples and the Coast." in Chittick, N. and Rothberg, R., *East Afica and the Orient*. New York: Africana Publishing Co. p. 216-225
Renfrew, C. (1972)
    The Emergence of Civilization: The Cyclades and the Aegean in the Third Millennium BC. London: Methuen.
Renfrew, C. (1975)
    Trade as Action at a Distance: Questions of Integration and Communication. In Sabloff, J and C.C. Lamberc-Karlovsky (eds), *Ancient Civilization and Trade*. p. 3-59. Albuquerque: University of New Mexico Press.
Renfrew, C and Bahn, P. (1991)
    Archaeology Theory and Methods. London: Thames and Hudson.

Sassoon, H. (1966)
   Guide to Kunduchi. Dar-es-Salaam: Antiquity Department.
Simpson, D. (1975)
   Dark Companions: The African Contribution to the European Exploration of East Africa. London: Paul Elek.
Sinclair, P. and T. Hakansson (2000)
   "The Swahili City-State." In Hansen, M. (ed.), *A Comparative Study of Thirty City-State Cultures*. Copenhagen: Reitzel Forlag, p. 463-482.
Soper, R. and Golden, B. (1969)
   "Archaeological Survey of Mwanza Region, Tanzania." *Azania* 4: 15-79.
Stanley, H. (1878)
   Through the Dark Continent. New York: Harper and Brothers.
Sutton, J. (1970)
   "Dar-es-Salaam: A Sketch of a Hundred Years." *Tanzania Notes and Records* 71: 1-20.
Sutton, J. (1998)
   "Kilwa: A History of the Ancient Swahili Town With a Guide to the Monuments of Kilwa Kisiwani and Adjacent Islands." *Azania* 33: 113-169.
Temple, P. (1971)
   "Discussion of C.S. Alexander's Paper on Marine Terraces of the Northeast Coast of Tanganyika." *Zeitschrift für Geomophologie* 15: 236-40.
Vernet, T. (2002)
   "Slave Trade: le Commerce des Esclaves sur la Côte Swahili, 1500-1750." *Azania* 38.
Versteijnen, Fr. C. (1968)
   The Catholic Mission of Bagamoyo. A.K. Zuber $ COD Saarbrücken.
Wheatley, P. (1975)
   "Analecta Sino-Africana Resensa." In Chittick, N. and Rothberg. R. (eds), *East Africa and the Orient*. New York: AfricanaPublishing Co. p. 76-114.

INDEX